Anonymous

The Constitution, Code of Statutes and Supplement

of the Grand Encampment of Knights Templar of the United States, and

the Statutes and General Regulations of the Grand Commandery of

California

Anonymous

The Constitution, Code of Statutes and Supplement
of the Grand Encampment of Knights Templar of the United States, and the
Statutes and General Regulations of the Grand Commandery of California

ISBN/EAN: 9783337219680

Printed in Europe, USA, Canada, Australia, Japan

Cover: Foto ©ninafisch / pixelio.de

More available books at **www.hansebooks.com**

THE

CONSTITUTION,

CODE OF STATUTES AND SUPPLEMENT,

OF THE

Grand Encampment

OF

Knights Templar of the United States,

AND THE

STATUTES AND GENERAL REGULATIONS

OF THE

⇒|GRAND ✳ COMMANDERY|⇐

OF

CALIFORNIA.

SAN FRANCISCO:

FRANK EASTMAN & CO., PRINTERS, 509 CLAY STREET.

1884.

CONSTITUTION

OF THE

Grand Encampment of Knights Templar

OF THE

UNITED STATES OF AMERICA.

1877.

ARTICLE I.

THE GRAND ENCAMPMENT—OF WHOM COMPOSED.

SECTION 1. The Grand Encampment of Knights Templar of the United States consists of the following members :—

(1.) The Grand Master.
The Deputy Grand Master.
The Grand Generalissimo.
The Grand Captain General.
The Grand Prelate.
The Grand Senior Warden.
The Grand Junior Warden.
The Grand Treasurer.
The Grand Recorder.
The Grand Standard Bearer.
The Grand Sword Bearer.
The Grand Warder.
The Grand Captain of the Guard—

the first nine of whom, (except the Grand Prelate,) shall be elected by ballot, and the remaining five shall be appointed by the Grand Master.

(2.) All Past Grand Masters.
All Past Deputy Grand Masters.
All Past Grand Generalissimos, and
All Past Grand Captains General of the Grand Encampment.

(3.) All Grand Commanders.
All Past Grand Commanders.
All Deputy Grand Commanders.
All Grand Generalissimos, and
All Grand Captains General of each Grand Commandery acknowledging the jurisdiction of the Grand Encampment ; each of whom shall be entitled, when present,

to one vote, and no more, (except as proxy,) in all the proceedings of the Grand Encampment.

(4.) The first three officers of each Commandery holding its charter immediately from the Grand Encampment, who, or as many of whom as may be present at any Conclave of the Grand Encampment, shall be entitled, collectively, to one vote.

SECTION 2. All officers of the late General Grand Encampment shall rank and have all the privileges of members of equal rank, as provided for herein.

SECTION 3. No persons shall be eligible to any office in the Grand Encampment, unless he shall be at the time a member of some subordinate Commandery, under the general or immediate jurisdiction of the Grand Encampment.

PROXIES.

SECTION 4. The first four officers named in the first Section ; the first four officers of Grand Commanderies, and the first three officers of subordinate chartered Commanderies, held under the immediate jurisdiction of the Grand Encampment, may appear and vote by *proxy;* said proxy being, at the time of service, a member of a subordinate Commandery, and producing a properly authenticated certificate of his appointment.

TITLES.

SECTION 5. The title and designation of the Grand Master of the Grand Encampment of the United States, is *Most Eminent Grand Master of Knights Templar.*

That of the Deputy Grand Master, *Right Eminent.*

That of the remaining officers of the Grand Encampment, *Very Eminent.*

CONCLAVES.

SECTION 6. A Grand Conclave of the Grand Encampment shall be held triennially, at such time and place as may have been previously designated by the Standing Committee, and approved by the Grand Encampment.

SECTION 7. Special Conclaves may be called by the Most Eminent Grand Master, at his discretion. And it shall be his *duty*, upon the requisition of the majority of the Grand Commanderies, to him directed in writing, to call a special Conclave.

SECTION 8. No business shall be transacted at a special Conclave, except that which was specified in the original summons.

POWERS AND DUTIES.

SECTION 9. 1. The Grand Encampment, at its regular Conclaves, shall review and consider all the official reports of its officers, and the proceedings of the Grand Commanderies and subordinate Commanderies under its immediate jurisdiction, for the preceding three years.

2. It shall elect by ballot its several officers, except the Grand Prelate, Grand Standard Bearer, Grand Sword Bearer, Grand Warder and Grand Captain of the Guard, who shall be appointed by the Grand Master, to serve during his term of office.

3. It shall adopt such Rules and Edicts as may be necessary for the good of the Order.

4. It shall examine the accounts of the Grand Treasurer and Grand Recorder.

5. It shall supervise the condition of the finances, and adopt such measures in relation thereto as may be necessary to increase, secure and preserve the same, and also to insure the utmost fidelity and punctuality on the part of every accounting officer, in the safe keeping and paying over the funds and property of the Grand Encampment.

6. It may grant or withhold warrants, dispensations and charters for new Grand or subordinate Commanderies.

7. For good cause, it may revoke pre-existing warrants, charters or dispensations.

8. It shall assign the limits of the Grand Commanderies, and settle all controversies that may arise between them.

9. And finally, it shall consider and do all matters and things appertaining to the good, well-being and perpetuation of the principles of Templar Masonry.

SECTION 10. At every Conclave, all questions shall be determined by a majority of votes, the presiding officer being entitled to one vote. In case the vote is equally divided, he has the casting vote.

SECTION 11. This Grand Encampment being a legislative body, acknowledging no superior, admits an appeal to be taken by any member from the decision of the chair on any question under consideration therein : *Provided, however*, that such appeal shall not be maintained unless two-thirds of all the members present shall vote therefor.

This rule is adopted for this Grand Encampment alone, and is not to be construed as establishing a precedent for the guidance of any other Masonic Body.

TENURE OF OFFICE.

SECTION 12. The officers of the Grand Encampment shall hold their respective offices until their successors shall be duly elected and installed.

THE GRAND MASTER.

SECTION 13. It is the prerogative and duty of the Grand Master, generally to exercise, as occasion may require, all the rights appertaining to his high office, in accordance with the usages of Templar Masonry.

And as a part thereof, he shall have a watchful supervision over all the Commanderies, Grand and subordinate, in the United States, and see that all Constitutional Enactments, Statutes and Edicts of the Grand Encampment are duly and promptly observed.

And that the work and discipline of Templar Masonry everywhere, are uniform throughout the jurisdiction of the Grand Encampment ; and that the dress is uniform, unless otherwise ordered by the Grand Encampment.

Among his special duties and prerogatives, are the following :—

1. To appoint the Grand Prelate, Grand Standard Bearer, Grand Sword Bearer, Grand Warder, Grand Captain of the Guard, to serve during his term of office.

2. To visit and preside in any Commandery, Grand or subordinate, in the United States, and give such instruction or directions as the good of the Order

may require, always adhering to the Constitution, Statutes and Edicts of the Grand Encampment.

3. To cause to be executed, and securely preserve and keep, the official bonds of the Grand Treasurer and Grand Recorder.

4. To grant Letters of Dispensation, during the Recess of the Grand Encampment, for the institution of new Commanderies, such dispensation to be in force no longer than the next Triennial Conclave of that body, and promptly to notify the Grand Recorder of the issuing of said Letters of Dispensation.

5. To grant warrants during the recess of the Grand Encampment for the institution of Grand Commanderies in States, Districts or Territories, where the same have not been heretofore established.

6. To manage and control his contingent fund.

THE DEPUTY GRAND MASTER.

SECTION 14. The Deputy Grand Master, in the event of the death, removal or physical incompetency of his superior, shall act as the Grand Master. At all other times he shall perform such duties as may be assigned him by the Grand Encampment or the Grand Master.

THE GRAND GENERALISSIMO AND GRAND CAPTAIN GENERAL.

SECTION 15. In the absence of their respective superiors, the Grand Generalissimo and Grand Captain General shall severally act as Grand Master, in order, according to rank. At all other times they shall perform such duties as may be assigned them by the Grand Encampment, or such as are traditionally appropriate to their respective stations.

THE GRAND TREASURER.

SECTION 16. 1. The Grand Treasurer, unless otherwise directed by the Grand Encampment, shall invest, from time to time, all such moneys as may come to his hands, belonging to the Grand Encampment, over and above the sum of three hundred dollars, in such way as he may judge most to the interest of the Grand Encampment, but subject to call on thirty days' notice. And the same shall be at his command on the first day of the month preceding the Triennial meeting of the Grand Encampment.

2. He shall render to the Grand Encampment, at its Triennial Conclaves, a true and perfect account of his doings in this respect, together with an account of all moneys received, and the earnings thereon accrued from investments, and the amounts disbursed by him during the vacation.

3. Also a copy of the same to the Grand Master, by the first day of the month preceding the Triennial Meeting, to the end that the Grand Master may make such suggestions on account thereof as he may deem necessary.

4. He shall pay all drafts drawn upon the contingent fund by the Grand Master.

5. He shall carefully preserve, and render from time to time, as ordered, an inventory of all property belonging to the Grand Encampment entrusted to his keeping.

THE GRAND RECORDER.

SECTION 17. 1. The Grand Recorder shall collect and receive all the revenue of the Grand Encampment, and pay over the amount to the Grand Treasurer whenever it reaches the sum of one hundred dollars.

2. He shall render, annually, to the Grand Master and to the Grand Treasurer, copies of his accounts of all moneys received and paid to the Grand Treasurer—naming the sources from which they were received—bringing up said accounts to the first day of September ; *provided*, that in the year in which the Conclave is held, it shall be rendered the first day of the month preceding.

3. And also to the Grand Encampment, triennially, a general account of the same, with his expenditures of the "contingent fund" of his office.

4. He shall forward to each newly constituted Commandery, immediately upon receiving official notice that a dispensation has issued, a copy of this Constitution, together with whatever Statutes and Edicts are in force.

5. He shall report to the Grand Encampment, on the first day of each Triennial Meeting, the names of the Grand Commanderies, and of those Commanderies working under the immediate jurisdiction of the Grand Encampment, which have not complied with the requisition to furnish him with its full annual historical and financial returns for the use of the Grand Encampment.

6. He shall report annually, on the first day of September, *except* the year of the Grand Conclave, when it shall be a month preceding, to the Grand Master, the names of the Grand Commanderies, and those Commanderies working under the immediate jurisdiction of the Grand Encampment, which have not complied with the requisition to furnish its full annual historical and financial returns for the use of the Grand Master.

7. He shall open and keep a "Book of Templar Masonry," in which shall be entered, in appropriate columns, the following subjects :—

A. A Register of Commanderies—to contain—

I. 1. The date of issuing every warrant by the Grand Master for the forming of a Grand Commandery.

2. The date of issuing every dispensation for a subordinate Commandery, and—

3. The date of issuing every charter for a subordinate Commandery, granted by authority of the Grand Encampment since its origin (1816).

II. 1. The Roll of Officers of the "Great Priory of the United Orders of the Temple and Malta, in England and Wales."

2. The Roll of Priories and Officers of the "Great Priory of the United Orders of the Temple and Malta, for the Dominion of Canada."

B. A Register of Membership.

I. The Roll of Officers of the Grand Encampment, with their terms of service, etc., since the origin of the same.

II. 1. The roll of elective Officers of the Grand Commanderies, terms of service, etc., from the organization of each.

2. The Roll of Officers of the subordinate Commanderies working under the jurisdiction of the Grand Encampment.

3. With all the current changes resulting from dismissions, suspensions, expulsions and deaths.

C. Historical data, tending to complete the history of Templar Masonry in the United States.

I. To collect and bind in orderly volumes, a copy of all the proceedings of the Grand Encampment since its organization.

II. 1. To collect and bind in orderly volumes, copies of the proceedings of all the Grand Commanderies, from the organization of each.

2. To collect and bind in orderly volumes, copies of the By-Laws of all the Grand Commanderies.

3. To collect and bind in an orderly volume, impressions of the seals of all the Grand Commanderies.

III. 1. To collect and bind in orderly volumes, copies of the By-Laws of all the subordinate Commanderies working under the immediate jurisdiction of the Grand Encampment.

2. To collect and bind in an orderly volume, impressions of the seals of each subordinate Commandery working under the immediate jurisdiction of the Grand Encampment.

8. And he shall also make a triennial report to the Grand Encampment of his official acts.

THE REMAINING OFFICERS.

SECTION 18. The duties of the remaining Officers of the Grand Encampment are such as are traditionally appropriate to their respective stations, or such as may be assigned them by the Grand Encampment.

GENERAL PROVISIONS.

SECTION 19. The Grand Master, the Deputy Grand Master, the Grand Generalissimo, and the Grand Captain General, are severally authorized to visit and preside in any Commandery of Knights Templar throughout the jurisdiction of the Grand Encampment, and to give such instructions and directions as the good of the Institution may require, always adhering to the Constitution, Statutes and Edicts of the Grand Encampment.

SECTION 20. In the event of the absence of all the four principal officers of the Grand Encampment, the Past Grand Officers, according to rank and seniority of service, shall be empowered to preside.

SECTION 21. The Grand Treasurer and the Grand Recorder shall severally give bond, with sureties, in such form and to such an amount—but not less than double the estimated triennial receipts by either—as shall from time to time be determined by the Grand Master, who shall judge and approve the efficiency of such bonds and sureties, and who shall keep and preserve the same.

SECTION 22. Any Grand Officer, save as above accepted, coming into the receipt of money or property belonging to the Grand Encampment, shall forthwith remit the same to the Grand Recorder.

ARTICLE II.

GRAND COMMANDERIES—HOW CONSTITUTED.

SECTION 23. Whenever there shall be three or more Subordinate Chartered Commanderies instituted or holden under this Constitution, in any one

State, District, or Territory, in which a Grand Commandery has not been heretofore formed, a Grand Commandery may be formed, after obtaining the Warrant of the Grand Encampment.

SECTION 24. Its jurisdiction shall be the territorial limits in which it is holden.

SECTION 25. The Grand Commandery of Massachusetts and Rhode Island is recognized as holding jurisdiction over both those States.

OF WHOM COMPOSED.

SECTION 26. A Grand Commandery consists of the following members :—

    (1.) The Grand Commander.
          The Deputy Grand Commander.
          The Grand Generalissimo.
          The Grand Captain General.
          The Grand Prelate.
          The Grand Senior Warden.
          The Grand Junior Warden.
          The Grand Treasurer.
          The Grand Recorder.
          The Grand Standard Bearer.
          The Grand Sword Bearer.
          The Grand Warder, and
          The Grand Captain of the Guard.

The first nine of whom shall be elected by ballot, and the remaining four shall be elected or appointed, as the Grand Commandery may direct.

    (2.) All Past Grand Commanders.
          All Past Deputy Grand Commanders.
          All Past Grand Generalissimos, and
          All Past Grand Captains General, of the same Grand Commandery, so long as they remain members of the subordinate Commanderies under the same territorial jurisdiction.

    (3.) The Commander.
          The Generalissimo, and
          The Captain General of each subordinate Commandery working under the same Grand Commandery.

    (4.) All Past Commanders of the subordinate Commanderies working under the same Grand Commandery, so long as they remain members of subordinate Commanderies under the same territorial jurisdiction ; *Provided, however*, that when a Past Commander changes his membership to a subordinate of a different Grand Commandery, such Grand Commandery may elect him to membership therein to continue as long as he is a member of a subordinate Commandery under its jurisdiction.

Each of whom shall be entitled, when present, to one vote, and no more, (except as proxy,) in all the proceedings of the Grand Commandery.

SECTION 27. No person shall be eligible to any office in a State Grand

Commandery, unless he shall be at the time a member of some subordinate Commandery working under the same Grand Commandery.

PROXIES.

SECTION 28. Any officer specified in the twenty-sixth section, except Past Commanders, may appear and vote *by proxy*, said proxy being at the time of service a member of the same subordinate Commandery as his principal, and producing a properly authenticated certificate of his appointment.

TITLES.

SECTION 29. The title and designation of the Grand Commander of a State Grand Commandery, is *Right Eminent*.

That of Deputy Grand Commander, *Very Eminent*.

Of the remaining officers of the Grand Commandery, *Eminent*.

CONCLAVES.

SECTION 30. Each Grand Commandery shall hold a regular Conclave annually, at such time and place as it may direct.

SECTION 31. Special Conclaves may be called by the Grand Commander.

SECTION 32. No business shall be transacted at a Special Conclave except that which was specified in the original summons.

POWERS AND DUTIES.

SECTION 33. (1.) Each Grand Commandery, at its Annual Conclave, shall review and consider all the official reports of its officers, and the proceedings of its subordinates for the preceding year.

(2.) It shall elect by ballot its several officers ; *Provided*, that the Grand Standard Bearer, the Grand Sword Bearer, the Grand Warder, and the Grand Captain of the Guard, may be elected or *appointed*, as the Grand Commandery may direct.

(3.) It shall have power to adopt such Rules and Edicts, subordinate to the Constitutions and the Statutes of the Grand Encampment of the United States, as may be necessary for the good of the Order.

(4.) It shall examine the accounts of the Grand Treasurer and Grand Recorder.

(5.) It shall supervise the state and condition of the finances, and adopt such measures in relation thereto as may be necessary to increase, secure, and preserve the same, and also to secure the utmost punctuality on the part of every accounting officer in the safe keeping and paying over the funds and property of the Grand Commandery.

(6.) It may grant or withhold Dispensations and Charters for new Commanderies.

(7.) For good cause it may revoke any pre-existing Charter or Dispensation.

(8.) It may assign the limits of subordinate Commanderies within its own jurisdiction, and settle all controversies that may arise between them.

(9.) And finally, it shall consider and do all matters and things appertaining to the good, well-being, and perpetuation of Templar Masonry, but always subordinate to the Grand Encampment of the United States.

SECTION 34. At every Conclave, all questions shall be determined by a majority of votes, the presiding officer, for the time being, being entitled to one vote. In case the votes are equally divided, he shall also give the casting vote.

SECTION 35. No appeal shall lie to the Grand Commandery from the decision of the Grand Commander, *except* on questions arising as to the construction of the Rules and Edicts of the Grand Commandery.

TENURE OF OFFICE.

SECTION 36. The several Grand Officers shall hold their respective offices until their successors shall be duly elected and installed.

THE GRAND COMMANDER.

SECTION 37. (1.) The Grand Commander shall have a watchful supervision over all the subordinate Commanderies under his jurisdiction, and see that the Constitution, Statutes and Edicts of the Grand Encampment, and the Constitution, Rules and Edicts of his own Grand Commandery, are duly and promptly observed.

(2.) He shall have the power and authority, during the recess of his Grand Commandery, to grant Letters of Dispensation to nine or more petitioners residing within his jurisdiction, and possessing the constitutional qualifications empowering them to form and open a Commandery.

(3.) Such Dispensation shall be in force no longer than the next Annual Conclave of his Grand Commandery.

(4.) But no Letters of Dispensation for constituting a new Commandery shall be issued save upon the recommendation of the Commandery in the same territorial jurisdiction nearest the location of the new Commandery prayed for.

(5.) During the recess of his Grand Commandery, he may suspend from the functions of his office any officer of the Grand or subordinate Commandery, or arrest the Charter or Dispensation of a Commandery ; but in neither case shall such suspension affect the standing in the Order of such officer, or his membership in the Commandery. And he shall report his action in full therein to the next Conclave of the Grand Commandery for its final action.

(6.) He may visit and preside at any Commandery within the jurisdiction of his Grand Commandery, and give such instructions and directions as the good of the Order may require, always adhering to the Constitution, Statutes and Edicts of the Grand Encampment, and the Constitution, Rules and Edicts of his Grand Commandery.

(7.) It is his duty, either in person, or by proxy, to attend all Conclaves of the Grand Encampment, and to see that the Grand Recorder *promptly* discharges the duty enjoined in Section 40 (3).

THE DEPUTY GRAND COMMANDER.

SECTION 38. (1.) The Deputy Grand Commander, in the event of the death, removal, or physical incompetency of his superior, shall act as the Grand Commander. At all other times, he shall perform such other duties as may be assigned him by the Grand Commander or the Grand Commandery.

(2.) It is his duty, either in person, or by proxy, to attend all Conclaves of the Grand Encampment.

GRAND GENERALISSIMO AND GRAND CAPTAIN GENERAL.

Section 39. (1.) In the absence of their respective superiors, the Grand Generalissimo and Grand Captain General shall severally act as Grand Commanders, in order, according to rank. At all other times they shall perform such duties as may be assigned them by the Grand Commandery, or such as are traditionally appropriate to their respective stations.

(2.) It is their duty, either in person, or by proxy, to attend all Conclaves of the Grand Encampment.

THE GRAND RECORDER.

Section 40. (1.) The Grand Recorder shall make an annual communication to the Grand Recorder of each of the other Grand Commanderies, likewise to the Grand Master and the Grand Recorder of the Grand Encampment.

(2.) Said communication shall embrace the roll of Grand Officers, and such other matters as may conduce to the general good of the Order.

(3.) He shall forward to the Grand Recorder of the Grand Encampment, on or before the first day of July of each year, Annual Returns and Dues for his Grand Commandery. [As amended at Chicago, August 20, A. D. 1880.]

(4.) He shall also annually transmit to the Grand Master and Grand Recorder of the Grand Encampment of the United States copies of all its printed Proceedings, and of the Statutes, Rules and Edicts adopted by this Grand Commandery.

THE REMAINING OFFICERS.

Section 41. The duties of the remaining officers, as well as those above specified, shall be such as are traditionally appropriate to their respective stations, or allotted to them by the Grand Commandery, and corresponding as near as may be to those of the corresponding officers of the Grand Encampment of the United States.

GENERAL PROVISIONS.

Section 42. In the event of the absence of the first four officers of the Grand Commandery, the Past Grand Officers, according to the rank and seniority of service, shall be empowered to preside.

ARTICLE III.

SUBORDINATE COMMANDERIES—HOW CONSTITUTED.

Section 43. Each Grand Commandery shall have exclusive power *to constitute new Commanderies* within its jurisdiction.

Section 44. The Grand Encampment shall have exclusive power to constitute new Commanderies within any State, District or Territory, wherein there is no Grand Commandery regularly formed under the authority of the Grand Encampment.

OF WHOM COMPOSED.

SECTION 45. A subordinate Commandery consists of the following members :—

  (1.) The Commander.
    The Generalissimo.
    The Captain General.
    The Prelate.
    The Senior Warden.
    The Junior Warden.
    The Treasurer.
    The Recorder.
    The Standard Bearer.
    The Sword Bearer, and
    The Warder.

(2.) As many members as may be found convenient for work and discipline ; each of whom shall be entitled when present, to one vote in the proceedings of the subordinate Commandery.

TITLES.

SECTION 46. The title and designation of the Commander of a subordinate Commandery is *Eminent*.

CONCLAVES.

SECTION 47. The Stated Conclaves of a subordinate Commandery shall be held at least semi-annually, at such time and place as may be specified in the charter, or designated in the By-Laws of the Commandery.

SECTION 48. Special Conclaves may be called by the Commander.

SECTION 49. No business shall be transacted at the Special Conclaves except that which was specified in the original summons.

POWERS AND DUTIES.

SECTION 50. At every Conclave all questions shall be determined by a majority of votes, the presiding officer, for the time being, being entitled to one vote. In case the votes are equally divided, he shall also give the casting vote.

SECTION 51. No appeal shall lie to the Commandery from the decision of the Commander.

OFFICERS.

SECTION 52. The several officers shall hold their respective offices until their successors are duly elected and installed.

THE COMMANDER.

SECTION 53. (1.) The Commander has it in special charge to see that the By-Laws of his Commandery are duly observed, as well as the Constitution, Statutes, Rules and Edicts of the Grand Commandery, and of the Grand Encampment of the United States.

(2.) That accurate records are kept and just accounts rendered.

(3.) That regular returns are made to the Grand Encampment or Grand Commandery annually, and that the annual dues are promptly paid.

(4.) It is his duty, together with the Generalissimo and Captain General, either in person or by proxy, to attend all Conclaves of the Grand Encampment or of his Grand Commandery.

THE RECORDER.

SECTION 54. (1.) It shall be the duty of the Recorder of every subordinate Commandery, working under the immediate jurisdiction of the Grand Encampment,

(2.) To report annually to the Grand Recorder of the Grand Encampment, up to the first day of July, the roll of his officers and members, and the working roll of his Commandery. [As amended August 20, 1880.]

(3.) And to accompany the same with the amount of dues to the Grand Encampment ; *provided*, that in the year in which the Grand Conclave is held, these duties shall be reported a month preceding.

(4.) For failure herein, the Commandery so offending shall be subject to knightly discipline.

GENERAL PROVISIONS.

SECTION 55. In the event of the absence of the first three officers of the Commandery, the Past Commanders, according to seniority of service, shall be empowered to preside.

ARTICLE IV.

MISCELLANEOUS — DUES, FEES, AND FINANCES.

SECTION 56. The Grand Commanderies, in such manner as they may respectively determine, shall annually collect and pay to the Grand Recorder of the Grand Encampment an amount equal to *five cents* for each Sir Knight returned as a member of their respective subordinate Commanderies, at the Conclave of the Grand Commandery preceding July the first in each year. [As amended August 20, 1880.]

SECTION 57. This fund, with the returns of the Grand Commandery, shall be forwarded to the Grand Recorder of the Grand Encampment on *or before* the first day of July in each year. Returns and dues shall be forwarded the month preceding. [As amended August 20, 1880.]

SECTION 58. The fee for instituting a new Commandery shall not be less than ninety dollars.

SECTION 59. For every Knight Templar created in any Commandery, whilst under the immediate jurisdiction of the Grand Encampment, there shall be paid two dollars into the treasury of the Grand Encampment.

SECTION 60. The Grand Recorder of the Grand Encampment shall receive ten dollars as his fee for each charter issued, and five dollars for endorsing, under the seal of the Grand Encampment, the extension of a dispensation.

SECTION 61. The Grand Commanderies, respectively, shall possess authority, upon the institution of new Commanderies within their respective jurisdictions—

(1.) To require from the several Commanderies within their respective jurisdictions, such proportions of the sums received by them for conferring the orders ;

(2.) Also such sums in the form of annual dues from their respective members as may be necessary for supporting the Grand Commandery.

SECTION 62. No subordinate Commandery shall confer the Orders of Knighthood for a less sum than twenty dollars.

GRAND MASTER'S CONTINGENT FUND.

SECTION 63. There shall be a Contingent Fund of three hundred dollars placed to the credit of the Most Eminent Grand Master, on the books of the Grand Treasurer, at the close of each Triennial Conclave, out of which the Grand Master shall reimburse himself for his necessary cash expenses in the performance of his constitutional duties, and make a triennial report of the same to the Grand Encampment.

GRAND RECORDER'S CONTINGENT FUND.

SECTION 64. There shall be appropriated, at each Triennial Conclave of the Grand Encampment, a sufficient sum to be used by the Grand Recorder to meet the current expenses of the secretariat, of which he shall render an account at the succeeding Triennial Conclave.

ROYAL ARCH MASONS ONLY ELIGIBLE TO THE ORDER.

SECTION 65. (1.) No Commandery, Grand or subordinate, shall confer the Orders of Knighthood upon any one who is not a regular Royal Arch Mason, according to the requirements of the General Grand Chapter of the United States.

ORDER OF SUCCESSION.

(2.) The rule of succession in conferring the Orders of Knighthood shall be as follows : 1. The Knight of the Red Cross. 2. Knight Templar, and Knight of Malta.

COMMANDERY TO HAVE DISPENSATION OR CHARTER.

(3.) Every Commandery working in a State, District, or Territory, where there is a Grand Commandery, shall have a dispensation or charter from said Grand Commandery. And no Commandery hereafter to be formed or opened in such State, District, or Territory, shall be deemed legal without such dispensation or charter.

WITHOUT CHARTER, ALL TEMPLAR COMMUNICATION FORBIDDEN.

(4.) All Templar communication is interdicted between any Commandery working under the general or special jurisdiction of this Grand Encampment, or any member thereof, and any Commandery or member of such, that may be formed, opened, or holden in such State, District, or Territory, without such dispensation or charter.

SOJOURNER NOT ELIGIBLE TO THE ORDER.

(5.) It shall be deemed irregular for any Commandery to confer the Orders of Knighthood, or either of them, upon any sojourner, whose place of residence is within any State, District, or Territory in which there is a Commandery regularly at work, until the consent of the Commandery having territorial jurisdiction is first obtained.

DISCIPLINE FOR VIOLATION OF (5).

(6.) In the event of the violation of this interdict, the Commandery so offending shall be subject to knightly discipline, and be required to pay over to the Commandery having jurisdiction the amount of fees received for such admission.

VOW OF OFFICE.

(7.) The officers of every Commandery, Grand and Subordinate, before entering upon the exercise of their respective offices, shall take the following vow, viz.: "I, (A. B.), do promise and vow that I will support and maintain the Constitution and Code of Statutes of the Grand Encampment of Knights Templar of the United States of America."

PROXIES MAY CONSTITUTE.

(8.) The Grand Master of this Grand Encampment may issue his proxy to any Knight Templar in regular standing, authorizing him to constitute a subordinate Commandery which has received a charter; and any Commandery thus constituted shall be deemed regularly constituted.

READING OF THE JOURNAL.

SECTION 66. (1.) After the opening of the Grand Encampment, it shall be the duty of the Grand Recorder to read the journal of the last Triennial Conclave, unless such reading be dispensed with; and at the resumption of business in each successive morning session, the minutes of the preceding day shall also be read.

COMMITTEE ON CREDENTIALS.

(2.) A Committee on Credentials, consisting of three, shall be appointed by the Grand Master at the opening of the Grand Conclave, to report at the opening of the next session. *Provided*, that no Grand or Subordinate Commandery shall be reported as represented, nor shall its representatives be entitled to seats unless the dues shall have been paid and the returns filed in the Grand Recorder's office, *except* by a vote of the Grand Encampment. [*As amended August 20, 1880.*]

REPORTS OF GRAND OFFICERS.

(3.) After the report of this committee, the Grand Master, the Deputy Grand Master, the Grand Generalissimo, the Grand Captain General, the Grand Treasurer, and the Grand Recorder will successively read the reports of their doings during the preceding three years.

These reports shall be referred to the standing committee on the doings of Grand Officers, who may recommend the apportionment of such parts thereof to special or to such other of the standing committees as they may deem necessary.

STANDING COMMITTEES.

(4.) The standing committees shall be:
1. A Committee on the Doings of the Grand Officers.
2. A Committee on Finance.
3. A Committee on Dispensations and New Commanderies.
4. A Committee on Unfinished Business.
5. A Committee on Grievances.
6. A Committee on Templar Jurisprudence.
7. A Committee to designate the place of the next Triennial Conclave.

8. A Committee on Printing, consisting of the Grand Master, Deputy Grand Master, and Grand Recorder, who shall contract for the printing of the proceedings of each Triennial Conclave, and determine, in the absence of a vote of the Grand Encampment, what portion of the proceedings shall be printed, and the style in which it shall be done. [*As Amended August 20, 1880.*]

NEW BUSINESS.

(5.) While the several committees are preparing their reports, the new business may be acted upon ; and if any subject is brought forward requiring a reference to any standing or special committee, it shall be so referred forthwith.

All committees shall report as soon as convenient after their appointment.

SPEAK BUT ONCE.

(6.) No Sir Knight shall be allowed to speak more than once on the same subject, except to explain the meaning of some of his remarks, *unless* it be by special permission of the Grand Encampment first obtained.

ELECTION OF OFFICERS.

(7.) The Grand Encampment shall proceed to the election of officers for the ensuing three years, immediately after the opening of the first session on Thursday following the commencement of the Triennial Conclave.

EXEMPLIFICATION OF THE WORK.

(8.) It shall be the duty of the Grand Master at each Triennial Conclave, if time permit, to cause an exemplification of the work appertaining to the Orders of Knighthood before the Grand Encampment ; and also to correct officially all irregularities and discrepancies that exist.

AMENDMENTS.

SECTION 67. The Grand Encampment shall be competent, upon the concurrence of three-fourths of its members present at any regular Conclave, to revise, amend, and alter this Constitution.

Provided, however, that any member intending to submit a motion relative to a change of the Constitution, Statutes, or Rituals, shall give notice thereof in writing to the Grand Recorder, at least four months before the day on which the Grand Conclave shall be held at which such subject is to be discussed, and notice thereof shall be inserted in the summons ; otherwise no such motion shall be entertained.

Provided, further, that the proposed amendments may be modified in any manner by the Grand Encampment while the same is under consideration. No modification, however, shall be made not germain to the matter contained in the original proposed amendment.

CODE OF STATUTES

OF THE

Grand Encampment of Knights Templar

OF THE

UNITED STATES OF AMERICA.

Adopted in 1874.

I. APPEAL.

1. An expelled or suspended Knight has the right of appeal to his Grand Commandery.

2. EFFECT OF APPEAL. An appeal taken from expulsion, or indefinite suspension, does not suspend the judgment appealed from. In other cases an appeal operates as a *supersedeas*.

3. If the judgment appealed from be reversed, the Knight who was under discipline is thereby restored to good standing and membership in his Commandery.

4. A Grand Commandery, upon an appeal, may modify the judgments of its subordinates.

5. If the Grand Commandery shall restore an expelled or suspended Knight to good standing merely, the Grand Recorder shall give a certificate to that effect.

6. An appeal taken and abandoned leaves the judgment in full force.

7. APPEAL, HOW HEARD. A Grand Commandery acting upon an appeal may admit the appellant to argue his own case, although he may have been expelled by his Commandery.

8. An accused may be represented by counsel at all stages of the trial: *provided*, such counsel shall be a Knight Templar in good standing.

9. APPEAL FROM THE GRAND COMMANDERY. A decision of a Grand Commandery is final, and no appeal to the Grand Encampment can be taken, *unless* the decision involves a construction of the Constitution, Code of Statutes or Edicts, or Statutes of the Grand Encampment.

II. ABSENTEES—RIGHTS OF.

A member of a Commannery has the right to know all the transactions at the Conclaves of his Commandery, whether affecting himself or not.

III. ADJOURN.

The Grand Encampment and Grand Commanderies "*adjourn.*"

IV. ASSESSMENTS.

1. MAY BE LEVIED. A Commandery, Grand Commandery, and the Grand Encampment, respectively, has the right to levy and collect such *pro rata* assessments as may be needed to pay the expenses of the body.

2. In the absence of any special law, a majority vote may determine the propriety of an assessment and the amount thereof ; *provided*, however, a member of a subordinate Commandery may appeal to his Grand Commandery if he feels aggrieved by such assessment, and claims that it is in violation of Templar law.

V. BALLOT.

1. To BE SECRET. The ballot upon a petition for the Orders, or for membership, must be secret, and it must be sacred ; and it can be taken only at a stated Conclave, unless by written permission of the Grand Commander.

2. WHO IS TO VOTE. Every member present when a ballot is taken is required to vote, unless excused by the Commandery before the balloting has commenced.

3. WHEN IT MAY BE REPEATED. An Eminent Commander, upon good cause shown, may order one reballot before the result of the ballot has been recorded, and before any member of the Commandery has left the asylum.

OBJECTIONS TO. See title "*Objection after Ballot.*"

VI. BUSINESS.

WHERE AND WHEN TRANSACTED. All business of the Commandery must be transacted in the asylum, and at a stated Conclave, or at a special Conclave, due notice of such Conclave and of the business to be transacted having been given to each member of the Commandery. Arrangements for the funeral of a Knight may be made and the Orders may be conferred at special Conclave.

VII. BURIAL.

1. RITUAL FOR. When a Knight is buried by his Commandery the burial ceremony approved by the Grand Encampment in 1859 must be observed.

2. RIGHT OF. An unaffiliated Knight Templar is not entitled to the honors of Knightly burial.

3. WHEN BY LODGE. A Commandery may perform escort duty at the burial of a Knight by his Lodge, when so requested.

VIII. CHARTER.

1. NECESSITY OF WARRANT OF GRAND MASTER. A Grand Commandery cannot be constituted without the warrant of the Grand Master, although the Grand Encampment has authorized its formation.

2. A subordinate Commandery cannot be constituted without a duly executed charter.

3. LOSS OF. If a Commandery should lose its charter, the Grand Commander can authorize it to hold Conclaves and transact business by issuing an order setting forth the facts ; which order shall have the effect of a charter until a duplicate shall be issued by the Grand Commandery.

4. WHEN IT MAY BE SURRENDERED. No Commandery can surrender its charter so long as there are nine members of the Commandery who desire and are able to work under said charter, according to the constitution of the Grand Commandery.

5. WHEN SURRENDERED OR ARRESTED, STATUS OF MEMBERS. When the charter of a Commandery shall have been surrendered or arrested, the members thereof in good standing shall, upon payment of their dues to the Grand Commandery, be entitled, on proper application, to a certificate of such good standing from the Grand Recorder having charge of the books and effects of the Commandery; *provided*, however, in case of the arrest of the charter, the Grand Commander may suspend, and the Grand Commandery may prohibit the issuing of such certificates to those whose actions or neglect of duty may have caused the arrest of the charter.

6. SURRENDERED AND RESTORED. A charter surrendered or arrested cannot be granted to form a new Commandery, but may be restored to the former members in good Templar standing who are unaffiliated.

7. In this case it is not proper to constitute the Commandery again.

IX. COMMANDERIES.

1. REQUISITES FOR FORMING. A dispensation or charter to form a new Commandery cannot be granted except upon a petition of at least nine Knights Templar in good standing.

2. Petitioners for a new Commandery need not dimit from other Commanderies.

See title "*Membership, Petitions,*" etc.

3. The petition for a dispensation must have indorsed upon it the recommendation of the Commandery nearest the location designated for the new one.

4. If the new Commandery is to be stationed in a city where there is more than one Commandery, two of those located in such city must recommend the petition.

See title "*Meetings—where held.*"

5. TRAVELING COMMANDERIES. No dispensation or charter can be granted to organize a traveling or itinerant Commandery.

6. UNDER DISPENSATION. A Commandery under dispensation cannot be constituted.

7. EXTINCT COMMANDERIES CANNOT BE REVIVED. When a Commandery U. D. ceases to exist it cannot be revived.

8. OFFICERS OF, NOT TO BE ELECTED OR INSTALLED. Its officers cannot be elected or installed.

9. CANNOT BE REPRESENTED. It cannot be represented in a Grand Body.

10. JURISDICTION OF. Except as above specified, it has the same rights and powers as a chartered Commandery.

11. STATUS OF KNIGHTS CREATED IN. Knights created in a Commandery U. D. are members thereof, and sustain the exact relation to that Commandery and to other Templars which is sustained by those knighted in chartered Commanderies.

12. HOW AFFECTED BY THE FORMATION OF GRAND COMMANDERIES. When a Grand Commandery is formed in a jurisdiction in which there is a Com-

mandery U. D., the latter comes at once under the authority of the former, and should report to it, and obtain from it or its Grand Commander a continuance of its dispensation.

13. How CREATED. A Commandery is created by the grant of a charter, which is the proper evidence of the fact, and becomes effective only when the Commandery shall have been constituted under it.

See title "*Charter—*(1.) *Necessity of warrant of Grand Master.*"

14. No Commandery shall be constituted until it is provided with a suitable asylum, properly furnished.

15. When constituted, report thereof should be made to the Grand Master or Grand Commander (as the case may be) and the Grand Recorder.

16. OFFICERS OF—WHEN TO BE INSTALLED. The officers can only be installed after the Commandery shall have been duly constituted in the presence of at least nine of its members.

17. The officers of a Commandery which has not been constituted are not members of the Grand Commandery, and cannot vote therein, although the charter of their Commandery has been issued.

18. DUTY WHEN GRAND COMMANDERY IS FORMED. Upon the formation of a Grand Commandery, it is the duty of every subordinate within its jurisdiction to enroll itself under such Grand Commandery, have its charter indorsed thereby, and to obey its Constitution and Statutes.

19. CAN BELONG TO NO OTHER GRAND COMMANDERY. A subordinate Commandery cannot be under the authority of, or belong to, any Grand Commandery but the one having jurisdiction over the State, Territory or District in which it is located.

20. FAILURE TO MEET—EFFECT OF. A Commandery failing to meet for twelve consecutive months forfeits all of its rights as a Commandery, and its charter should be arrested.

21. DISSOLUTION OF A GRAND COMMANDERY—EFFECT OF. If a Grand Commandery should dissolve, its subordinates do not for that cause cease to exist, but pass at once under the immediate authority of the Grand Encampment.

22. WHEN MAY APPEAR IN PUBLIC. Commanderies shall not appear in public, as such, without permission of the Grand Commander, except upon funeral occasions.

23. When Commanderies appear in public, in their own State or out of it, they are under the immediate authority of the Grand Commander if he chooses to assume the command. If he is not present, the officer upon whom under the Constitution his duties devolve, may act in his place. But all are under the authority of the Grand Commander in whose jurisdiction they may, at the time, be.

COMMANDERIES ILLEGAL. See title "*Illegal Commanderies.*"

JURISDICTION OF. See title "*Jurisdiction.*"

24. HOW CONCLAVES TERMINATE. Subordinate Commanderies " close ;" they do not " call off," or " adjourn."

See title "*Adjourn.*"

CHARTER MUST BE PRESENT. See title "*Warrant.*"

UNIFORM OF. See title "*Uniform.*"

X. CONFER ORDERS—WHO CAN.

In the absence of the Eminent Commander, the Generalissimo, and in the absence of both, the Captain General, and in the absence of all three, the Past Commander, according to the seniority of service, may preside and confer the Orders of Knighthood. (As amended in 1877. See proceedings, p. 172.)

COSTUME.

See title "*Uniform.*"

XI. DEBATE.

How CLOSED. When the presiding officer wishes the debate to close he rises, and that ends the discussion.

XII. DECISIONS.

DECISIONS OF GRAND MASTER, ETC., TO BE DIGESTED. All decisions of the Grand Master, as approved or modified by the Grand Encampment, and all decisions of the Grand Encampment, to be digested and published as a Supplement to the Code of Statutes. The digest to be made by a "special committee." (See proceedings 1877, pp. 182, 186.)

XIII. DIMITS.

How GRANTED. A member of a Commandery may receive a dimit without a vote of the Commandery, at a stated Conclave, upon request made in the open Commandery; *provided*, his dues shall have been paid, and no charges are pending against him.

EFFECT OF. See titles "*Rank of Officers,*" "*Burial.*"

XIV. ELECTIONS.

1. How HELD. All elections, in all Templar bodies, must be by ballot.

2. BLANKS VOID. Blanks are not votes, and cannot be considered as such in the elections of officers.

XV. EMINENT COMMANDER.

1. How SUSPENDED. An Eminent Commander may be suspended by his Grand Commander, or the officer acting as such, in his own State, or out of it with his Commandery; and this suspension continues until revoked by the Grand Commander, or reversed by trial. But suspension from office does not affect his membership in his Commandery.

2. TRIAL OF. An Eminent Commander cannot be tried by his own Commandery, but by the Grand Commandery, and by the Grand Encampment where there is no Grand Commandery.

XVI. EXTINCT COMMANDERIES.

1. How MAY BECOME SO. See titles "*Commanderies--Failure to Meet: Charter—When Surrendered,*" etc.

2. How REVIVED. See title "*Charter—Surrendered and Restored.*"

3. REVIVED, NOT TO BE CONSTITUTED. See title "*Charter—Surrendered and Restored.*"

4. STATUS OF MEMBERS OF. When a Commandery has ceased to exist, its members may join another Commandery, upon petition, and certificate from

the Grand Recorder of the State holding the charter and papers of the extinct Commandery, that his standing therein was good when said Commandery ceased to exist.

5. CHARTER, WHEN IT MAY BE SURRENDERED. See title "*Charter—When it may be*," etc.

XVII. EXPULSION OR SUSPENSION.

1. BY COMMANDERY—EFFECT OF. The suspension or expulsion of a Knight by his Commandery deprives him of all the rights and privileges of Knighthood so long as the judgment remains in force.

2. BY LODGE OR CHAPTER. Expulsion or suspension from his *Masonic rights* by his Lodge or Chapter, deprives a Knight of all rights and privileges in his Commandery, and of all intercourse with the Order.

3. In such case a certificate of the Lodge or Chapter, of its action, must be filed with the Recorder of the Commandery, and a minute should be made of the reception of such certificate, and of its legal effect, to-wit: that the Knight is thereby divested of his knightly rank and of all its privileges.

4. The certificate from the Lodge or Chapter must show not only the fact of suspension or expulsion, but also that the body had jurisdiction.

5. If a certificate of the facts cannot be obtained from the Secretary of the Lodge or Chapter, they may be proved by oral testimony; and the same entry should be made as required in paragraph 3.

6. When the expulsion or suspension is made or confirmed by the Grand Lodge or Grand Chapter, as the case may be, the Commandery cannot go behind the record or adjudicate upon the question of jurisdiction.

7. HOW REMOVED. A Knight who has been expelled by his Commandery may be restored by a two-thirds vote to good standing.

8. If suspended by his Commandery, a majority vote will restore to good standing.

9. In either case of suspension or expulsion by his Commandery the Knight can be restored to membership only upon petition and unanimous ballot.

10. When the suspension or expulsion from the Commandery was the result of suspension or expulsion by Lodge or Chapter, a certificate of his restoration in the body which disciplined him will restore the Knight to good standing and membership.

11. In case of definite suspension, the restoration of the Knight to his Lodge or Chapter restores him to knightly standing.*

XVIII. FEES.

CANNOT BE REMITTED. The prescribed fees for the Orders of Knighthood cannot be remitted by a Commandery, directly or indirectly.

XIX. FOREIGN KNIGHTS.

NOT RED CROSS. A Knight Templar created in a foreign jurisdiction, and who has not received the Order of Red Cross, may, at his examination, take the vow and have that Order communicated to him, and thereafter may be admitted to the asylum.

FOREIGN REPRESENTATIVES. See title "*Representatives*," etc.

---

* NOTE—See Digest, "Expulsion and Suspension."

XX. GRAND COMMANDERIES.

1. HOW FORMED. A Grand Commandery can be formed only in a State, Territory or District where none exists, and only upon the petition of at least three chartered Commanderies.

2. The warrant of the Grand Master is necessary, although the Grand Encampment may have authorized a warrant to be issued.

3. Each subordinate Commandery must be represented, and there must be at least nine members present.

4. When a warrant is duly issued, a convocation of the representatives of at least three of the petitioning Commanderies is held ; the warrant of the Grand Master is read ; credentials are examined and approved ; a resolution is adopted agreeing to form a Grand Commandery ; a Code of Statutes is adopted, and officers are elected and installed. All of these proceedings must be entered upon the journal, and due report thereof made to the Grand Master and Grand Recorder of the Grand Encampment.

5. The Commanderies rank according to the dates of their Charters ; and the Eminent Commander of the oldest Commandery is, by courtesy, entitled to command or preside until a Grand Commander is elected and installed.

6. WHEN GRAND COMMANDERY CEASES TO EXIST. A Grand Commandery once formed continues to exist as long as it has nine members : when the number of its constitutional members becomes less than nine it becomes extinct.

XXI. HEALING.

1. Healing consists in re-obligating the Knight, and correcting what has been done amiss at his creation.

2. BY WHOM. The Grand Commandery or Grand Commander, (by its authority) in whose jurisdiction a Knight was irregularly created, has power to heal him.

3. This power may be delegated to a subordinate Commandery or an Eminent Commander.

4. WHO CANNOT BE HEALED. One Knighted in a clandestine manner or in a spurious Commandery cannot be healed.

HONORARY MEMBERS.

See title " *Membership—Honorary.* "

XXII. ILLEGAL COMMANDERIES.

WITHOUT DISPENSATION OR CHARTER. All Commanderies or pretended Commanderies are spurious unless held under a Dispensation or Charter as herein prescribed ; and all communication with such bodies is forbidden, and also all recognition and intercourse with their members as Knights.

XXIII. INFORMATION.

HOW OBTAINED. Knights desiring information relative to any point in law or usage of Templar Masonry, should apply to their Eminent Commander ; the Eminent Commander, if necessary, shall apply to his Grand Commander, and the Grand Commander, in turn, to the Grand Master.

XXIV. INSTALL OFFICERS.

1. OF GRAND ENCAMPMENT—WHO MAY. The officers of the Grand Encampment may be installed by the Grand Master, or by a Past Grand Master. If none such are present, then by the oldest Past Grand Commander (by service) who may be present.

2. OF GRAND COMMANDERY. The officers of a Grand Commandery may be installed by either of the first four officers of the Grand Encampment, by a Past Grand Master, by the Grand Commander, or by a Past Grand Commander. If none such are present, then by the oldest Past Eminent Commander (by service) who may be present.

3. OF A SUBORDINATE COMMANDERY. The officers of a subordinate Commandery may be installed by any permanent member of the Grand Encampment, by either of the first four officers of the Grand Commandery, by the Eminent Commander, or by a Past Eminent Commander. The ceremony used in such case shall be that prescribed by the Grand Encampment in the "Forms for Installation." [As amended 1877. See Supplement.]

4. WHEN TO BE. The officers of a new Commandery cannot be installed at the Conclave of the Grand Commandery at which the Charter is granted, unless the Commandery shall have first been legally constituted, and such officers shall have been duly elected.

5. When installation is performed by one in office, no special authority is required.

6. WHEN BY PROXY. When by a past officer, the commanding officer must be present authorizing it, or his written proxy must be produced.

7. The officers to be installed cannot be represented by a proxy.

OFFICERS U. D. NOT TO BE. See title "*Commanderies Under Dispensation.*"

8. WHEN BY COMMISSION. Officers-elect of the Grand Encampment, or of a Grand Commandery, who cannot be present at the regular time for installation, may be installed in such Commandery as the Grand Encampment or Grand Commandery respectively may designate.

9. The Recorder of the Commandery in which such installation shall take place shall forthwith certify the fact to the Grand Recorder.

XXV. JURISDICTION.

1. BOUNDARIES OF. In the absence of a Statute of the proper Grand Commandery, or of a Special Edict of the Grand Encampment, defining the limits of each Commandery, the jurisdiction thereof, whether chartered or under dispensation, extends in all directions to one-half the distance, by a direct line, between itself and the next nearest Commandery: *Provided*, that in no case can it extend beyond the limits of the State, Territory or District in which it is located.

2. Each Commandery has penal jurisdiction over all Knights non-affiliated, as well as affiliated, for violation of moral or Templar law within its territorial jurisdiction.

3. VIOLATION OF. It is not lawful for a Commandery to confer the Orders upon any one residing within the jurisdiction of another Commandery, without first obtaining the permission of such Commandery.

4. OVER SOJOURNERS. When a petition for the Orders is received from a sojourner, or from one who has not resided for six months within the jurisdiction of the Commandery, it is the duty of the Commandery receiving it to notify the Commandery within whose jurisdiction the petitioner resided, and obtain its consent that jurisdiction shall be exercised over the petition of the petitioner.

5. It shall be competent, in such cases, for a Commandery to waive its jurisdiction, and permit another Commandery to confer the Orders upon one residing within its jurisdiction.

XXVI. MEETINGS.

1. WHERE HELD. A Commandery can hold its Conclaves only in the place designated in its Dispensation or Charter.

2. A Commandery may remove its asylum from one house to another in the same place, by a vote of a majority of its members present at a stated Conclave, and after due notice of the proposed change.

3. If the regular asylum of a Commandery, from any cause, becomes an unfit or improper place for holding the Conclaves, the Grand Commander may authorize them to be held elsewhere in the same place.

FAILURE OF. See title "*Commanderies—Failure to Meet.*"

XXVII. MEMBERSHIP.

1. WHO ARE MEMBERS OF A COMMANDERY. Those who receive the Order of the Temple in a Commandery are *ipso facto* members thereof, whether such Commandery be chartered or under dispensation.

2. PETITIONERS FOR A NEW COMMANDERY—STATUS OF. After a Dispensation is granted to form a new Commandery the membership of the Knights who petitioned therefor remains in abeyance as to the older Commanderies to which they belonged when signing the petition. They become active members of the Commandery while under dispensation, and when a Charter is granted, and the Commandery constituted, they continue to be members of the new Commandery, and cease to be members of the old ones.

3. If the Dispensation should be withdrawn, or a Charter refused, the Knights who petitioned therefor resume their membership in their former Commanderies without petition or other ceremony.

4. When a Charter is granted, and the Commandery constituted, the Recorder of the new Commandery must certify the fact to each Commandery to which any of the petitioning Knights belonged, and this will terminate their former affiliation.

5. HONORARY. Honorary membership does not confer the right to vote, nor any rank or standing therein, but is merely complimentary.

XXVIII. OFFICERS.

1. INCOMPATIBLE. When any one of the first three officers of a Commandery shall be elected and installed as Grand Master or Grand Commander, his rights and powers as such subordinate officer, for the time being, *ipso facto*, ceases, and the vacancy shall be filled as hereinafter provided for. (See proceedings 1877, p. 174.)

2. SUCCESSION OF. When a vancy occurs in the office of Eminent Commander, the powers and duties devolve upon the Generalissimo, and if there should be no Generalissimo, upon the Captain General.

3. When there is no officer in line to fill a vacancy, the commanding officer shall, by appointment, fill the vacancy pro tem.

4. If a vacancy occur in any elective office other than that of Eminent Commander, the Grand Commander may authorize a new election, upon re-request to that effect by the Commandery: Provided, however, in case of a vacancy in both the offices of Eminent Commander and Generalissimo, the Captain General shall succeed to the duties and powers of the Eminent Commander, without an election.

5. When the vacancy is in one of the appointive offices, it shall be filled by appointment by the commanding officer.

6. FAILURE TO BE INSTALLED. If any officer duly elected or appointed shall, without reasonable excuse, neglect to attend at the time fixed for installation, his election or appointment may be declared void by a vote of the body which elected him, or by the officer who appointed him.

7. CHANGE OF RESIDENCE, EFFECT OF. Whenever a Grand Commander or an Eminent Commander changes his residence to a place beyond the jurisdiction of his Grand Commandery, he thereby vacates his office, and can exercise its powers no longer.

RANK OF. See title "Rank—Of Officers."

WHO MAY RESIGN. See title "Resign."

XXIX. OBJECTION AFTER BALLOT.

1. WHO MAY MAKE. A member of a Commandery in good standing may object to the conferring of the Orders upon an elected candidate, and this whether the objecting Knight was present when the ballot was taken or not.

2. When such objection is made, either in open Commandery or to the Eminent Commander, the Orders cannot be conferred ; and the fact of objection alone, and not the name of the objector, should be entered upon the minutes, and it is equivalent to the rejection of the candidate by ballot.

3. The objecting Knight cannot be required to disclose his reasons therefor.

4. OF VISITING KNIGHTS. Objections to a candidate may be received from a visiting Knight, and should be duly considered by the Commandery ; but they are not conclusive, like those of a member.

XXX. PETITION FOR ORDERS.

1. FORM OF. Every petition for the Orders of Knighthood shall declare the Lodge and Chapter in which the petitioner received the degrees, and shall state whether he has or has not been previously rejected by any Commandery.

2. It shall also declare that the petitioner is a firm believer in the Christian religion.

3. MUST BE SIGNED. No petition can be received unless signed by the applicant in person, giving his full name, residence and occupation.

4. BUT ONE APPLICANT TO SIGN A PETITION. No petition can be received which is signed by more than one applicant.

5. To be recommended. Each petition must be signed by two vouchers and recommenders, who are members of the Commandery to which the petition is presented.

6. Cannot be withdrawn. When a petition has been presented to a Commandery it cannot be withdrawn, unless it shall appear that the Commandery has not jurisdiction over the petitioner.

7. Report not to be recorded. The character of the report of a committee of inquiry, whether favorable or unfavorable, should never be recorded.

8. Unfavorable report, effect of. An unfavorable report does not dispense with the necessity of a ballot, which must be taken in all cases.

9. When to be received and acted on. Petitions can be received or acted on only at stated Conclaves, *unless* by written permission of the Grand Commander.

10. No ballot can be had upon a petition until after it has been referred to a committee of three members of the Commandery, and that committee has reported.

11. A petition cannot be balloted on until at least four weeks after it has been presented to the Commandery, *unless* by written permission of the Grand Commander.

See title "*Ballot—to be Secret.*"

12. When a rejected petition may be renewed. The petition of one who has been rejected cannot be renewed until at least six months after such rejection.

13. Where. It may then be received by the Commandery in whose jurisdiction the petitioner then resides: *Provided*, the Commandery by which he was rejected consents to waive its jurisdiction.

Prelate in Red Cross. See title "*Red Cross—High Priest.*"

XXXI. PROXY.

In Grand Bodies. No person can give or act as proxy except those upon whom the power is conferred in the Constitution.

Officers cannot be installed by. See title "*Install Officers—when by proxy.*"

Installing officer may grant, when. See title "*Install Officers—when by commission.*"

XXXII. QUALIFICATION FOR ORDERS.

What required. See title "*Petition for Orders—form of.*"

1. Council Degrees, etc., not necessary. It is not necessary that petitioners should have received the degrees of Royal and Select Master.

2. Nor is it necessary that the petitioner be a member of either Lodge or Chapter.

3. Loss of a leg, etc., effect of. The loss of a leg or arm by a petitioner disqualifies him from receiving the Orders of Knighthood.

XXXIII. QUORUM.

What constitutes. A quorum in the Grand Encampment, Grand Commanderies and subordinate Commanderies, consists of nine members entitled to vote therein, including an officer entitled to open the body.

XXXIV. RANK.

1. OF COMMANDERIES, GRAND AND SUBORDINATE. Commanderies, Grand and subordinate, take rank according to the date of their several organizations, unless any of them voluntarily waive their proper rank.

2. OF OFFICERS. Election (or appointment) and installation are necessary to confer rank.

3. The Standard Bearer outranks the Sword Bearer, and the Sword Bearer outranks the Warder, and the Treasurer outranks the Recorder.

4. Present officers on duty in their own bodies outrank past officers of any grade.

5. A Knight dimitting to the jurisdiction of another Grand Commandery forfeits his membership and right to voice and vote in the Grand and subordinate Commandery of which he had been a member, and acquires no rank in the Grand Commandery of the jurisdiction in which he has affiliated, but "a Past Commander may be elected to membership therein."

6. But Past Grand Commanders do not lose their membership in the Grand Encampment by change of membership to another jurisdiction, nor by becoming unaffiliated.

7. HONORARY MEMBERSHIP. Honorary membership confers no rank.

XXXV. RESIGN.

1. WHO MAY RESIGN. Any officer of a Commandery under dispensation may resign, with the consent of the Grand Master or Grand Commander, respectively.

2. Neither of the first three officers of a chartered Commandery can resign after installation.

REPEATING THE BALLOT. See title "*Ballot—when it may be repeated.*"

XXXVI. RED CROSS.

FROM FOREIGN COUNTRIES. See title "*Foreign Knights.*"

HIGH PRIEST, NOT PRELATE. In the Council of Red Cross Knights "High Priest" is the title of the officer ministering at the altar.

REVIVAL OF OLD CHARTER. See title "*Charter—Surrendered and Restored.*"

XXXVII. REPRESENTATIVES.

FOREIGN, NOT TO BE APPOINTED BY GRAND COMMANDERIES. Grand Commanderies cannot exchange representatives with Templar organizations outside of the jurisdiction of the Grand Encampment of the United States.

XXXVIII. RITUAL.

NOT TO BE ALTERED. The ritual as promulgated by the Grand Encampment cannot be altered or abridged by the Grand Master, Grand Commander, or Grand Commandery.

BURIAL. See title "*Burial—Ritual for.*"

FOR INSTALLATION. See title "*Install Officers,*" etc., and forms adopted by the Grand Encampment.

XXXIX. SEAL.

FORM OF, ADOPTED. The seal of the Grand Encampment is that adopted September 12, 1844 (see reprint, p. 95), and altered September 15, 1856 (reprint, p. 311), and affixed to the Constitution, edition 1856, and Attestation, 1877.

XL. SUMMONS.

1. WHAT IS LEGAL.   A notice published in the newspapers is not a legal summons ; it must be by personal service, or by notice left at the residence or place of business of the person summoned, or deposited in the post office, directed to his usual address.

2. SEAL NECESSARY.   It is necessary that the seal should be affixed to a summons, but not to a notice of a Conclave.

3. KNIGHTS SHOULD OBEY.   Every Knight should promptly and strictly obey the summons of his Commander.

4. CONTAIN NOTICE, ETC.   All propositions to amend Code, etc., must be inserted in the summons to attend Triennial Conclave.

SUSPENSION.   See title *"Expulsion or Suspension."*

XLI. TITLE.

WHAT CONSTITUTES.   One who has filled by election and a term of service an elective office retains the rank and title, with the word " Past" prefixed—as Past Eminent Commander, Past Grand Commander, Past Grand Master.

OF PRELATE.   See title *"Red Cross—High Priest."*

XLII. TRIAL.

1. HOW CONDUCTED.   Trials of Sir Knights shall be in open Commandery; and the Eminent Commander shall preside, and decide all questions of law and all questions upon the admissibility of evidence.   And the trial shall be conducted as prescribed in the " Forms for Templar Trials," enacted and promulgated by the Grand Encampment.

2. When a trial takes place in the Grand Commandery, the Grand Commander shall preside ; when in the Grand Encampment, the Grand Master shall preside.

See titles *"Appeal—How heard ;" "Eminent Commander—Trial of."*

XLIII. UNAFFILIATED KNIGHTS.

CANNOT VOTE.   Unaffiliated Knights cannot vote in person or as proxy, or hold office in any Commandery, Grand or subordinate.   They are, however, amenable for violation of moral or Templar law to the Commandery within whose jurisdiction they reside.

EFFECT OF DIMIT.   See titles *"Burial—Right of ;" "Rank—Of Officers ;" "Dimit—Effect of."*

CANNOT HAVE KNIGHTLY BURIAL.   See title *"Burial—Right of."*

XLIV. UNIFORM.

1. OF KNIGHTS TEMPLAR.   The uniform of a Knight Templar is that prescribed by the Grand Encampment in 1862.   No other uniform is allowed, and no authority other than the Grand Encampment can modify or alter it.

2. *Provided,* however, that all members of Commanderies which now have what is known as the " black uniform" be permitted to wear it while members of said Commandery ; but no other Commandery, nor the members thereof,

shall be authorized or permitted to wear any other than the regulation prescribed in 1862.

3. *Provided, further,* that any Commandery in a State where the black uniform is worn may, by permission of its Grand Commandery, adopt and wear such black uniform.

4. No officer or member can be present in the Grand Encampment, or in a Grand Commandery, unless in full Templar uniform, except by vote of the body excusing him.

5. OF KNIGHTS OF THE RED CROSS. The Templar baldric reversed, exhibiting the green side; Templar cap covered; sword, and white gloves; constitute the uniform of a Red Cross Knight. The Sovereign Master wears the royal robes and crown, and the High Priest his full robes, etc.

OF KNIGHTS OF MALTA. Same as Knights Templar.

UNDER DISPENSATION—COMMANDERY. See title *"Commanderies—Under Dispensation."*

VACANCIES—HOW FILLED. See title *"Officers—Succession of."*

XLV. VISITING KNIGHTS.

OBJECTION OF A MEMBER EXCLUDES. No visiting Knight can be admitted to an asylum if one only of the regular members present objects. The objection may be made openly or privately to the Eminent Commander, and in neither case can the objector be required to disclose his reasons for his objection.

XLVI. WARRANT OR DISPENSATION.

MUST BE PRESENT. The dispensation or charter of a Commandery must always be present at the opening and throughout the Conclave.

SUPPLEMENT TO THE CODE OF STATUTES

OR

DIGEST OF TEMPLAR LAW

OF THE

⇥ GRAND ENCAMPMENT OF KNIGHTS TEMPLAR ⇤

OF THE

UNITED STATES OF AMERICA.

CONTAINING A DIGEST OF THE DECISIONS OF THE CONCLAVES OF A. D., 1874, 1877, 1880 AND 1883, MADE BY SIR KNIGHT JOSIAH H. DRUMMOND, MAINE, THE SPECIAL COMMITTEE.

ADVANCEMENT.

See *Objection after Ballot*, 92, 92a.

AMENDMENTS.

1. Proposed amendments to the Constitution or Code, of which notice is given in the summons, may be acted upon by the Grand Encampment in the absence of the proposer.   1877.

APPEAL.

1a. The appeal of a Sir Knight from the action of the Eminent Commander of his Commandery, although in the pursuance of an order of the Grand Commander, lies to the Grand Commandery, and not to the Grand Master. 1883.

ASSESSMENTS.

2. An assessment for social entertainments cannot be enforced against one not participating.   1874.

BALLOT.

3. After a candidate has been declared rejected and the fact recorded, the ballot cannot be repeated, even to correct an alleged mistake.   1880.

4. A ballot cannot be taken upon a petition at the same Conclave at which it is presented, without a dispensation from the Grand Commander, even by a unanimous vote of the Commandery.   1880.

4a. In Commanderies under the immediate jurisdiction of the Grand Encampment, the Grand Master may, by dispensation, authorize the reception of a new petition from a rejected candidate within less than six months after the rejection ; and is the exclusive judge of the propriety of granting such dispensation.   1883.

See *Petitions*, 97, 99.

5. The books of the Grand Treasurer and Grand Recorder shall be submitted, at each Conclave, for the inspection of the Finance Committee. 1877.

BY-LAWS.

6. A by-law fixing annual dues and providing that members in arrears for two years shall be ineligible to office and not entitled to vote, and that their names may be dropped from the rolls subject to be reinstated on payment of arrearages by a majority vote, is valid. 1874.

7. But a member should be disfranchised only after due trial, and the by-laws should make provision therefor. 1877.

8. A by-law providing that a member, upon the payment of a fixed sum of money, may become a life member and thereafter be exempt from annual dues, is valid. 1880.

9. A by-law requiring a Red Cross Knight to equip himself with a uniform before he can receive the Order of the Temple is valid. 1880.

CHARTER.

10. The Eminent Commander, and no other, is the legal custodian of the charter of the Commandery. 1880.

CHRISTIAN KNIGHTHOOD.

10a. The ritual contains those things which a Knight obligates himself to believe and perform. The Grand Master has no authority to give additional definitions. 1883.

COMMANDERY.

11. The funds and property of an extinct Commandery become the property of the Grand Commandery, which may make such disposition thereof as it deems proper. 1877.

12. It is improper for a Commandery to " call off " from one Conclave to another; but it may close to meet on another day to finish business that is pending. 1874.

13. A Commandery "of the indispensable number" may be authorized by a Grand Commander or Grand Commandery, as well as by the Grand Master or Grand Encampment. 1874.

14. A Commandery requires no dispensation or permission to change to a "mounted Commandery." 1880.

15. *Affiliated* Sir Knights, petitioning for a new Commandery, are not required to file their dimits with the Grand Recorder; but *non-affiliated* petitioners must do so. 1880.

15a. A Commandery cannot confer the Orders upon a candidate elected by another Commandery, at the request of such other Commandery, without a dispensation. 1883.

See *Grand Commandery,* 69.

COMMANDERIES U. D.

16. The provision requiring the recommendation of the nearest Commandery in order to form a new one does not apply to dispensations granted by the Grand Master, who has absolute power in the premises. 1874.

17.   A Commandery U. D. requires no formal proceedings in order to commence work.   The members assemble and proceed as if regularly constituted.
1877.

18.   Their officers ordinarily hold office during the continuance of the dispensation ; but the Grand Master [or Grand Commander] has the power to relieve an officer and appoint another.   1874.

19.   Such dues may be collected from the members as the majority of the Commandery may determine.   1874.

20.   Any signer of the petition for a dispensation, by consent of the officer granting the same, and of the Commandery, may dissolve.his connection with it ; and, thereupon, his membership revives in.his old Commandery.   1874.

21.   The petitioners for a dispensation become charter members unless they have severed their connection with the Commandery U. D. [or their names are omitted from the charter by action of the Grand Commandery].   1877.

22.   It is not proper to name the officers in the charter of a new Commandery.   1874.

23.   It can be constituted only by the Grand Master, or the Grand Commander, or his duly appointed proxy.   1874.

24.   It cannot elect officers until it has been constituted ; to save time, however, at the constitution of the Commandery, it is not improper to agree upon the officers in advance, and have a merely *formal* election at that time.
See *Dispensation,* 37a; *Quorum,* 108a; *Dues,* 40a.   1874.

COMMITTEES (STANDING) APPPOINTED IN ADVANCE.

25.   The Grand Master is authorized to appoint the Committee on Templar Jurisprudence at each Conclave, to act during the recess and at the succeeding Conclave.   1877.

26.   And the remaining of the standing committees sixty days previously to each Conclave, notifying the Grand Recorder of said appointments.   1877.

27.   The decisions of the Grand Master shall be referred to the Committee on Jurisprudence.   1877.

28.   The Grand Recorder shall place the financial and all other reports and official papers in the hands of the chairman of the proper committee [under the direction of the Grand Master] thirty days previous to the Conclave.
1877.

29.   The several committees so appointed shall have their reports ready for submission to the Grand Encampment the first day of its Conclave.   1877.

COMPLAINTS.

30.   Complaints should be made in the first instance to the Eminent Commander, and through him to the Grand Commander, and through him to the Grand Master, if the latter has any jurisdiction in the case.   Other communications should go through the same channel, save in special cases, when the officer refuses to act.   1874.

CORRESPONDENCE.

31.   It is proper for the Grand Master to correspond through one of his staff with a Grand Commander.   1877.

32.   Correspondence between subordinates of different Grand Commanderies should be forwarded through their respective Grand Commanders.   1877.

32*a*. Correspondence between a Commandery under the immediate jurisdiction of the Grand Encampment and a subordinate to a Grand Commandery should be through the Grand Master and the Grand Commander. 1883.

DECISIONS.

33. The decisions of a Grand Commander are binding on his subordinates as soon as known ; and an officer who has positive knowledge of such decision is as much bound by it as if it had been delivered directly to him. 1877.

33*a*. The decision of a Grand Commander, which his Grand Commandery refuses to approve, is of no binding force after such refusal. 1883.

33*b*. A member of a Commandery under the immediate jurisdiction of the Grand Encampment, in applying to the Grand Master for a decision, must do so through his Eminent Commander. 1883.

33*c*. Questions by members of a Commandery subordinate to a Grand Commandery, or by a Deputy Grand Commander, or a Past Grand Commander, should be submitted to the Grand Commander. 1883.

See *Committees*, 27.

DIMIT.

34. When, upon application by a member, the Commandery votes to grant him a dimit, the vote severs the membership, whether a certificate issues or not. 1880.

35. Application for a dimit must now be made in writing, signed by the member desiring it. 1880.

See *Commandery*, 15 ; *Restoration*, 118.

DISPENSATION.

36. The Grand Commander has the power to grant a dispensation to act upon a petition in less than four weeks after its presentation, although the by-laws of the Commandery make no such exception. 1880.

37. Such dispensation can be asked for only by vote of the Commandery ; but a majority vote is sufficient. 1880.

37*a*. When a dispensation for a new Commandery has been refused for any cause, the matter can be revived only by a new petition. 1883.

DUES.

38. A Commandery cannot exempt a member from all yearly dues by a vote to that effect, or by electing him an honorary member. 1877. 1880.

39. A member of an extinct Commandery is not liable for dues after the Commandery becomes extinct. 1880.

40. But the Grand Commandery has the right to collect from members of an extinct Commandery all dues chargeable against them up to the time it became extinct, and to discipline those who refuse or neglect to pay the same. 1880.

40*a*. When a member of a chartered Commandery becomes a member of a Commandery U. D., and continues paying dues to the former, it is not liable to pay to the latter the amounts so received, nor is the Sir Knight freed from his liability to pay dues to the Commandery U. D. 1883.

See *Membership*, 78 ; *By-Laws*, 68.

EMINENT COMMANDER.

41. When an Eminent Commander vacates his office, by having been elected and installed Grand Commander, or in any other manner, the Generalissimo (or in his absence the Captain General) succeeds to the office by constitutional right until the next annual election, and the Grand Commandery cannot legally order or authorize the election of a new Commander to fill the vacancy.   1880.

42. An Eminent Commander becomes a Past Commander at the expiration of his term of office, although he may have permanently removed from the State before that time.   1880.

EXPULSION AND SUSPENSION.

43. It requires a two-thirds vote to expel, but only a majority vote to suspend.   1880.

44. When a Templar is expelled or suspended by his Lodge or Chapter, the Code requires that a proper certificate thereof be obtained if practicable ; but if not, that other evidence be produced to the Commandery, showing the expulsion or suspension, before the Commandery can declare him expelled or suspended.   1880.

45. When the expulsion or suspension is the act of a subordinate Lodge or Chapter, its jurisdiction should be inquired into by the Commandery before final action.   1880.

46. But if the expulsion or suspension is decreed or confirmed by the Grand Lodge or Grand Chapter, the question of jurisdiction is no longer open.   1880.

47. Expulsion or suspension has the same effect, whatever may have been the cause for which it was inflicted.   1880.   1883.

48. In paragraph eleven of Section XVII of the Code of 1877, the word "definite" before "suspension" was accidentally omitted ; the term means "suspension for a definite time."   1880.

49. Suspension for non-payment of dues, by the Lodge or Chapter, has the effect given to it by the laws of the Grand Lodge or Grand Chapter of the jurisdiction ; it depends upon those laws whether all *Masonic rights* are taken away, or certain disabilities are incurred. Templar rights are taken away in the former case, but not necessarily in the latter.   1874.   1883.

50. But striking from the roll, without trial, is not suspension.   1874.   1883.

51. Striking from the roll of membership by the Lodge or Chapter affects the standing of the Sir Knight in the Commandery precisely the same as it does in the Lodge or Chapter.   1880.   1883.

52. Suspension for non-payment of dues can be inflicted by the Commandery only after due notice to the delinquent to appear at the time it is proposed to act upon his case, and an opportunity to be heard in his defence ; and any by-law providing for suspension without such notice and opportunity is illegal and void.   1877.   1880.

53. Suspension by Lodge or Chapter does not deprive his Commandery of jurisdiction to try him for other offences committed either before or after his suspension.   1877.

53*a*. Expulsion or suspension from the rights of Freemasonry by his Lodge or Chapter deprives a Sir Knight of all rights and privileges in his Commandery and of all intercourse with the Order.   · 1883.

53*b*. When members of a Commandery are summoned to show cause why they should not be suspended, and do not appear, the Eminent Commander cannot declare them suspended until the Commandery has so voted.   1883.

See Striking from the Roll.

FEES.

54. The fees for the Orders cannot be remitted directly, or indirectly by vote of money to the candidate.

55. No custom, however long it has existed, justifies the conferring of the Orders upon any one without the payment of the prescribed fees.

FUNERAL.

56. A Commandery cannot appear in public at the funeral of any other than a Templar, without the permission of the Grand Commander.

1877. 1880.

57. It is not proper for a Commandery, as escort, to attend the funeral of any one who is not buried with Masonic ceremonies.   1877.

GOOD STANDING.

58. A member of a Commandery is affected by his standing in his Lodge and Chapter.   1880.

59. A candidate not in good standing in Lodge and Chapter is not eligible to receive the orders of Knighthood.   1880.

60. The forfeiture or surrender of the charter does not, of itself, affect the good standing of the members.   1880.

See *Expulsion and Suspension*, 49, 51 ; *Membership*, 86 ; *Non-affiliates*, 89 ; *Reinstatement*, 112 ; *Restoration*, 114, 116, 118 : *Striking from the Roll.*

GRAND COMMANDERY.

61. To form a Grand Commandery, at least three Commanderies must be represented in the convention ; but Past Commanders may participate in the convention, and be counted in making the required number of Knights.

· 1877.

62. The membership of a Grand Commandery cannot be enlarged, or restricted from that prescribed by the Constitution of the Grand Encampment. .

1874.

63. Any member of a subordinate Commandery is eligible to office in the Grand Commandery.   1874.

64. A member can have but one vote in his own right in a Grand Commandery, nor can he vote personally in one capacity and by proxy in another.

. 1874.

64*a*. This rule applies to an officer or permanent member of the Grand Commandery, who is at the same time one of the first three officers of his Commandery.   1883.

65. Hence an officer of a subordinate Commandery, although the others are absent, cannot [in the Grand Commandery] cast more than one vote, unless he holds the duly authenticated proxies of the absent officers.   1877.

66. No person, other than those named in the Constitution of the Grand Encampment as members of a Grand Commandery, can vote therein in his own right, by virtue of any authority whatever, nor as proxy of any other than a member of his own Commandery, who, under the provisions of that Constitution, is a member of the Grand Commandery, and authorized to appoint a proxy.   1874.

67. No one can be appointed upon a committee in the Grand Commandery unless he is a member thereof in his own right or as proxy ; but a member may be appointed, though not present.   1880.

68. A non-resident of the State is not eligible to office in the Grand Commandery   1880.

69. Any officer of the Grand Commandery, except the Grand Commander, may be tried by his Commandery for unknightly conduct.   1880.

See *Rank*, 110, 111.

GRAND MASTER.

69*a*. The Grand Master, as the executive head of the Grand Encampment is, by the general principles of Masonic and Templar law, responsible for the discharge of every executive duty to be performed in behalf of the Grand Encampment not by enactment devolved upon others.   1883.

69*b*. It is not his duty to pass upon merely moot questions; but only those which actually arise in the administration of the affairs of the Grand Encampment, Grand Commanderies, or subordinate Commanderies.   1883.

GRAND OFFICERS.

69*c*. The Grand Master or his representative, the Deputy Grand Master, Grand Generalissimo, and Grand Captain General of the Grand Encampment, when visiting a body of the Order, are entitled to be received under the Arch of Steel.   1883.

69*d*. The Grand Encampment has not prescribed the manner of receiving the officers of a Grand Commandery, and any regulation made by a Grand Commandery in relation thereto is binding on the members of its obedience.
                                                                                            1883.

INSTALLATION.

70. It is not necessary for a re-elected officer to be installed, as he holds over, by virtue of his former election and installation, until his successor is installed.   1877.

71. A Commandery may hold a public installation in its own asylum, without a special dispensation from the Grand Commander.   1880.

72. But such dispensation is required in order to hold a public installation in any other place.   1880.

JEWEL OF PAST GRAND MASTER.

73. The form of the Jewel prepared for Past Grand Master FELLOWS [see Proceedings, with engraving] is adopted as the appropriate Jewel of a Past M∴ E∴ Grand Master of Knights Templar of this Grand Encampment.
                                                                                            1877.

JURISDICTION.

I. *Territorial.*—74. The jurisdiction of a Commandery [except when otherwise specially provided] extends half-way to the nearest Commandery in the same jurisdiction ; and a Commandery U. D., while its dispensation is in force, has the same jurisdiction as a chartered Commandery.　　1874.

75. A Companion, residing in any Territory in which there is no Commandery, may apply to any Commandery for the Orders ; but when there is a Commandery in such Territory he can apply elsewhere only by its permission, the Grand Master having no power in the premises.　　1874.

II. *Personal.*—76. A rejected candidate cannot apply to another Commandery, without the consent, by a unanimous vote, of the one by which he was rejected.　　1877.

77. The same rule applies to an elected candidate who fails to present himself to receive the Orders.　　1877.

MEMBERSHIP.

78. A Templar cannot be a member of two Commanderies at the same time, although they are not in the same State.　　1880.

79. An unaffiliated Knight is not entitled to Templar honors ; but the Commandery may grant them, or it may withhold them, without breach of knightly duty.　　1874.

80. The "honorary membership" named in the Code refers to the election, as an honorary member, by one Commandery, of the member of another.

1877.

81. Such honorary member is not liable to dues, and the election confers no rights, being a mere compliment.　　1880.

82. The election of a member of the same Commandery as an honorary member deprives him of none of the rights of active membership.　　1877.

83. Nor does it relieve him from the payment of dues.　　1880.

84. A plan of life membership approved. See Proceedings of 1874, page 50.　　1874.

85. A by-law providing that a member, upon the payment of a fixed sum of money, may become a life member, and thereafter be exempt from the payment of annual dues, is valid.　　1880.

86. When a Templar, after suspension and restoration to good standing, applies for membership, he must do so by petition, setting forth that he had been a member of a Commandery, been suspended, and restored to good standing : such petition [if in the same Commandery] need not lie over, but may be acted upon at once.

86*a.* Affiliation is a thing wholly between the applicant and the Commandery.　　1883.

See *By-Laws*, 8 ; *Restoration*, 115, 117.

MEMBERSHIP IN GRAND ENCAMPMENT.

- 86*b.* The election [and installation] of a Sir Knight as a Grand Commander make him a member of the Grand Encampment.　　1883.

86*c.* Documents distributed by the Grand Encampment to its members do not belong to the proxies attending the Grand Encampment, but to the members themselves.　　1883.

MINUTES.

87.   At the close of every Conclave, the minutes should be read, corrected, and approved ; they should be entered on the record before the next stated Conclave, when the journal should be read, corrected, and approved by the Commandery, and signed by the Recorder.   1874.

MONEYS—HOW PAID OUT.

88.   No money belonging to the Grand Encampment shall be paid out *except* upon a warrant or order signed by the Grand Master and attested by the Grand Recorder.   1877.

NON-AFFILIATES.

89.   By merely becoming non-affiliate in Lodge or Chapter, a Templar does not lose his standing in the Commandery.   1880.

OBJECTION AFTER BALLOT.

90.   An objection after ballot may be withdrawn before it has been entered on the minutes ; after that, the only course is to present a new petition in the same manner as if the rejection had been by ballot.   1877.

91.   Objection after ballot is in all cases equivalent to a rejection, whether the objector gives his reasons or not ; if he does give them, the Commandery has no right to determine their sufficiency.   1880.

92.   Objection to the advancement of a Red Cross Knight is equivalent to a rejection by ballot, and holds good for six months, and no longer.   1880.

92*a*.   Objection to the advancement of a Red Cross Knight is equivalent to a rejection by ballot, and-the money paid for the advancement should be returned to the candidate.   1883.

OFFICERS.

93.   By election and installation as Grand Commander, any one of the first three officers in a Commandery vacates his office. [See Code, "OFFICES— *Incompatible.*"]   1877.

94.   Section XXVIII of the Code applies to such a vacancy, in the same manner as it applies to other vacancies.   1877.

See *Eminent Commander*, 41 ; *Grand Commander*, 69.

PAST COMMANDER.

95.   A Past Commander, when presiding in the absence of the Eminent Commander, Generalissimo, and Captain-General, may confer the Orders.
1877.

95*a*.   The Past Commander who may preside in the absence of the first three officers of a Commandery is the *Senior* Past Commander present who is a member, without reference to the Commandery in which he acquired the title.
1883.

See *Eminent Commander*, 42.

PETITIONS.

96.   Petitions must contain what is prescribed by the Code of Statutes. No Commandery has the right to add new requirements.   1877.   1883.

97. They cannot be acted upon in less than four weeks from their presentation, without the special dispensation of the Grand Commander, even if the Commandery holds stated Conclaves weekly. 1877.

98. The report thereon must be in writing [but not entered upon the minutes], and the proper entry is "the committee, etc., presented their report, whereupon a ballot was had." 1877.

99. When the Eminent Commander has good reason to believe that there has been an error in announcing the acceptance of a candidate, he may, by ermission of the Grand Commander, order a new ballot, first giving notice, to all the members, of the time when it will be taken. 1877.

See *Ballot*, 3, 4.

PRINTING—COMMITTEE ON.

99a. The legislation of the Grand Encampment shows its intention that the printing should be under the supervision of its Committee on Printing. 1883.

99b. But the reprinting of the Proceedings 1859–1868 was made an exception to the rule, and intrusted to the Grand Recorder. 1883.

PRINTING REPORTS IN ADVANCE.

100. The Grand Recorder shall cause to be printed in advance of each Conclave a sufficient number of copies of the reports of the Grand Officers for the use of the committees and members, that each member present at the Conclave shall have a copy. 1871. 1877.

PUBLIC PARADES.

101. The Grand Encampment will accept no invitation to unite in a Templar parade during its Conclave. 1874. 1877.

102. It prohibits any of its members from participating therein during such Conclave, *except* to escort the Grand Encampment at the opening session of the Conclave. 1874. 1877.

103. The Grand Encampment requests the Grand Commandery within whose jurisdiction it may hold its Conclave, to prevent any Templar parade in the city where the Conclave is held on any day thereof after the first. 1874. 1877.

103a. A Commandery should appear in public in Templar costume only on Masonic occasions; and a dispensation for that purpose should be restricted to such an occasion. 1883.

103b. The determination of what is a Masonic occasion belongs to the Grand Lodge. 1883.

See *Funeral*, 56, 57; *Installation*, 71, 72.

QUALIFICATIONS FOR ORDERS.

104. If the candidate can give all the signs, and go through all the ceremonies, he is eligible, and not otherwise; and the Eminent Commander and the members of the Commandery are the judges of his eligibility under this rule. 1874.

105. But the Commandery should be more exacting than the Lodge or Chapter, and the petitioner should be capable of enduring pilgrimage and warfare, and should not by his presence mar the symmetry of a parade.   1877.

105a. The decision of the question whether a candidate can comply with the requirements of the ritual and drill is left to the Commandery.   1883.

106. No Commandery or Grand Commandery has the right to add to or take from the qualifications of candidates prescribed in the Constitution and Code of the Grand Encampment.   1877. 1880. 1883.

107. Hence the Council degrees are not prerequisite, and membership in Lodge or Chapter is not required. [See Code XXXII.]   1877.

107a. Hence, also, a candidate cannot be required to become a member of a Lodge or Chapter after receiving the Orders.   1883.

See *Good Standing*, 59.

QUORUM.

108. A quorum being present, the vote of a less number is valid.   1874.

108a. The law requiring nine members of the Commandery to be present in order to transact any business, applies to Commanderies U. D.

RANK.

109. A Past Grand Commander remains a member of the Grand Encampment as long as he is in good standing, whatever be his residence.   1880.

110. He remains a member of his own Grand Commandery as long as he is a member of one of its subordinates, whether he continues to reside in its jurisdiction or not.   1880.

111. But if he affiliates in another jurisdiction, he loses his membership in his own Grand Commandery, and does not acquire membership in that of his new affiliation until elected, as provided in Section XXVI of the Constitution of the Grand Encampment.   1880.

REINSTATEMENT.

112. When a member of a Commandery loses his good standing by being "stricken from the roll" by his Lodge or Chapter, his reinstatement in the Lodge or Chapter reinstates him in the Commandery.   1880.

RESTORATION.

113. The provisions of the Code, in relation to restoration, apply to cases of suspension for a *definite* time, as well as to suspension for an indefinite time.   1877.

114. The Grand Encampment has adopted the generally received law that the restoration, by his Lodge or Chapter, of a Templar expelled or suspended by such Lodge or Chapter, restores him to all the rights of which he was deprived by the Lodge or Chapter, viz., to good standing as a Templar, and to membership in his Commandery.   1880.

115. Under the law of the Grand Encampment, suspension, as well as expulsion, by the Commandery, severs membership therein.   1880.

116. A Sir Knight may be restored to good standing as an unaffiliated Knight by a majority vote when he has been suspended, and by a two-thirds vote when he has been expelled.   1880.

117. But in either case he can be restored to membership only by a unanimous vote.   1880.

118. When a suspended Sir Knight is restored to good standing, his Commandery should give him a certificate, stating that he had been a member, had been suspended [not stating the cause], and had been [at a given date], restored to good standing ; and such certificate would be equivalent to a dimit.   1880.

SEAL.

119. The officers of a Commandery have the right to order its seal affixed to any certificate or other documents which they can legally issue in the name of the Commandery.   1874.

STRIKING FROM THE ROLL.

119a. *Striking from the roll* is ordinarily not expulsion or suspension, but results in non-affiliation merely.   1883.

119b. If, however, *striking from the roll* of a Lodge or Chapter is held by its Grand Lodge or Grand Chapter to deprive the member of his *Masonic rights*, it has the same effect as expulsion or suspension.   1883.

119c. But if *striking from the roll*, under the law of the Grand Lodge or Grand Chapter of the jurisdiction, merely deprives the party of membership in his Lodge or Chapter, it has no effect upon the general standing of the Sir Knight, or his membership in his Commandery.   1883.

SUMMONS.

120. A summons in a subordinate Commandery should be used only in cases of urgent necessity.   1874.

TEMPLAR NOMENCLATURE.

121. The style "Sir Knight A B " is correct.   1880.

TITLE.

122. No past officers, except the presiding officer of a Grand or subordinate Commandery, retain their official title.   1877.

TRIALS.

123 Trials must take place in open Commandery, as provided in the Code. A committee may be appointed to take the depositions of such witnesses only as cannot be examined in open Commandery, to be returned to the Commandery.   1877.

124. But it is not proper to refer the charge to a committee for consideration ; nor for a committee, appointed to take testimony, to digest it or report any conclusions thereon.   1877.

UNIFORM.

125. The uniform is prescribed by a statute, and no Knight, Commandery, or Grand Commandery has any right to add to or take from *this* statute, any more than any other statute of the Grand Encampment.   1877.

126. All Past Grand Officers are entitled to wear the Templar Cross.   1874.

127. The wearing of shoulder-straps is limited to the officers and past officers enumerated in the statute.   1877.

128. The Grand Encampment cannot act upon any proposed change in the uniform, unless notice thereof is given in the summons, as provided in the Constitution. 1877.

128*a*. When a Commandery is entitled to wear the black uniform, new members as well as old may wear it.

128*b*. In the absence of any legislation by the Grand Encampment or the governing Grand Commandery, each Commandery may determine by its by-laws whether or not Sir Knights may be admitted to the sessions without full Templar uniform. 1883.

See *By-Laws*, 9.

VISITORS.

129. The objection of one member excludes a visitor, *unless* he visits in an official capacity. 1874.

130. A visitor must be examined in all the preceding degrees, as well as in the Order, *unless* vouched for in whole or in part. 1874.

VOTE.

131. By the Constitution of the Grand Encampment, all questions [*except* upon the acceptance, etc., of candidates, and in expulsions and restorations of Knights] are decided by a majority vote. 1874. 1880.

See *Expulsion and Suspension*, 43.

WORK—FORM OF MINUTE.

132. To change from the Commandery to the Council, the proper entry is, "The Commandery of Knights Templar was then closed, and a Council of Knights of Red Cross was opened;" and to change the other way, the entry is, "The Council of Knights of Red Cross was closed, and a Commandery of Knights Templar opened." 1877.

STATUTES

OF THE

Grand Commandery of Knights Templar

OF THE

STATE OF CALIFORNIA.

APRIL, A. D. 1884, A. O. 766.

—•◄•►•—

CHAPTER I.

RELATIVE TO THE GRAND COMMANDERY.

I.

Of its Title and Seal.

This Body shall be entitled "The Grand Commandery of Knights Templar of the State of California;" and shall have a Seal bearing suitable devices and inscriptions, which shall be affixed to all instruments issued by or under its authority.

II.

Of its Officers and Members.

The Grand Commandery shall be composed of a Grand Commander (whose address is *Right Eminent*); a Deputy Grand Commander (whose address is *Very Eminent*); a Grand Generalissimo; a Grand Captain General; a Grand Prelate; a Grand Senior Warden; a Grand Junior Warden; a Grand Treasurer; a Grand Recorder; a Grand Standard Bearer; a Grand Sword Bearer; a Grand Warder; (whose several addresses are *Eminent*); a Grand Organist; a Grand Captain of the Guards (the Sentinel); all Past Grand Commanders, Past Deputy Grand Commanders, Past Grand Generalissimos, Past Grand Captains General of this Grand Commandery; all Past Commanders, by service, of chartered Commanderies under its jurisdiction; and the Commanders, Generalissimos, and Captains General, for the time, of the several chartered and duly constituted Commanderies subordinate thereto.

III.

Of Qualifications for Office or Membership.

Every officer and member of the Grand Commandery must be a member of some Commandery under its jurisdiction : and with the suspension or cessation of such membership, shall cease his office and membership in the Grand Commandery.

IV.

Of its Powers and Authority.

The Grand Commandery derives all its powers from the Grand Encampment of Knights Templar of the United States of America, to the Constitution and Regulations of which its obedience is ever due. Under these powers it has authority over all Commanderies and Knights Templar within the State of California. It may grant dispensations and charters for forming and holding Commanderies therein, and, at its pleasure, may arrest, suspend, or revoke them. It may enact such statutes, and pass such orders, for its own government and for that of its subordinates and the Knights within its jurisdiction, as shall not conflict with the Constitution and Regulations of the Grand Encampment; may alter, amend, or annul the same ; and may exercise all other authority which shall be deemed necessary for the good of the Order in this State, and which shall be in conformity with its precepts and the Constitution and Regulations of the Grand Encampment. ·

V.

Of its Conclaves.

The Grand Commandery shall hold an Annual Conclave, for the transaction of its regular business, at the city of San Francisco, commencing on the first Thursday after the fourth Tuesday in April, at two o'clock P. M. Special Conclaves may be ordered by the Grand Commander, at his discretion, but no business shall be transacted thereat other than that specified in such order.

VI.

Of its Elections.

The Officers of the Grand Commandery shall be chosen by ballot at each Annual Conclave, (except the Grand Standard Bearer, the Grand Sword Bearer, the Grand Warder, and the Grand Captain of the Guards, who shall be appointed by the Grand Commander,) shall be duly installed before the close thereof, and shall hold their respective offices (except as hereinbefore provided) until their successors are elected, or appointed, and installed. A majority of all the votes cast shall be necessary for a choice. Any vacancy in office, occurring when the Grand Commandery is not in Conclave, may be filled by the Grand Commander, and the officer so appointed shall possess all the powers and be charged with all the duties of one regularly elected.

VII.

Of Proxies.

Any member of the Grand Commandery, except Past Commanders and the Grand Captain of the Guards, may appear and vote by proxy ; but such proxy must, at the time of service, be a member of the same Commandery as his principal, and must present a properly authenticated certificate of his appointment.

VIII.

Of Voting.

Each member of the Grand Commandery present shall be entitled to one vote, and all questions shall be determined by a majority of votes. In case the votes are equally divided, the Grand Commander, in addition to his proper vote, shall give the casting vote.

IX.

Of Revenue.

The revenue of the Grand Commandery shall be derived from fees charged for Dispensations, Charters, Diplomas and other instruments issued under its authority, as follows :—

1. For a Dispensation, one hundred and twenty-five dollars, of which fifteen dollars shall be the fee of the Grand Recorder ;

2. For a Charter, seventy-five dollars, of which fifteen dollars shall be the fee of the Grand Recorder ;

3. For a Diploma, five dollars, of which three dollars shall be the fee of the Grand Recorder ;

And from the following contributions levied upon the several Commanderies :

1. For each Order of the Red Cross conferred, two dollars ;

2. For each Order of the Temple conferred, three dollars ;

3. For each Knight Templar borne upon the rolls at the date of the annual returns, one dollar.

X.

Of Committees.

The following regular committees, to consist of three members each, shall be appointed by the Grand Commander at each Annual Conclave, viz.: on Credentials, on Reports of the Grand Officers, on Appeals and Grievances, on Jurisprudence, on New Commanderies, on Returns of Subordinates, and on Pay of Delegates. The Grand Commander may also appoint such special committees, at any Conclave, as may be deemed expedient by the Grand Commandery.

XI.

Of Finances and Accounts.

The Grand Commander, before the close of each Annual Conclave, shall also appoint a Committee on Finances and Accounts, which shall constitute a standing committee, and whose duty it shall be to meet at the office of the Grand Recorder, on the day preceding the Annual Conclave of the Grand Commandery, and examine the books, papers, and accounts of the Grand Recorder and Grand Treasurer, and report the result thereof to the Grand Commandery on the first day of the Annual Conclave in each year.

CHAPTER II.

RELATIVE TO THE GRAND OFFICERS.

I.

Of the Grand Commander.

The Grand Commander shall, at each Annual Conclave, present a written report of all his official acts during the year, and of the condition of the Order within his jurisdiction, together with such recommendations as he shall deem conducive to its prosperity and advancement. He shall have a watchful supervision over the subordinate Commanderies, and shall carefully see that the Constitution and Regulations of the Grand Encampment, and the Statutes and Orders of the Grand Commandery, are duly and properly observed. He shall have power, when the Grand Commandery is not in Conclave, to issue Dispensations for the formation of new Commanderies, as hereinafter provided ; and shall, either in person, or by proxy, constitute all new Commanderies, when chartered, and install their officers. He may, for good reasons shown, issue special dispensations to Commanderies, authorizing them to hold elections of officers at times other than that named in Statute IV, Chapter III, of these Statutes ; to receive and act again upon the petitions of rejected applicants for the Orders of Knighthood within a less period than the six months prescribed in Statute VI, of said Chapter III ; to ballot for and confer the Orders upon candidates, without the reference of their petitions to committees ; and to do such other things, not specifically provided for, as shall not be repugnant to, or inconsistent with the general regulations of the Order. He may order special Conclaves, at his discretion, specifying the object thereof. He may visit and preside in any Commandery within his jurisdiction, and give such orders and instructions as he may deem necessary, and as shall not be inconsistent with the enactments of the Grand Encampment and Grand Commandery. He may arrest the charter or dispensation of any Commandery, for good reasons shown, and for proper cause may suspend any Commander from the functions of his office until the next Annual Conclave. It shall be his duty, either in person or by proxy, to attend all meetings of the Grand Encampment ; and there shall be no appeal to the Grand Commandery from his decisions. He shall also exemplify, or cause to be exemplified, the ritual and drill of the Order at each Annual Conclave. He may also summon the Commander, Generalissimo, and Captain General of each Commandery, to meet him at any convenient place within the jurisdiction, for the purpose of exemplifying the drill and ritual, and the necessary expenses of these officers shall be paid by their respective Commanderies.

II.

Of the Deputy Grand Commander.

The Deputy Grand Commander, in the absence of the Grand Commander from any Conclave, shall take command ; and in the event of the death, absence from the State, or inability to serve, from any cause, of the Grand Commander, he shall succeed to and be charged with all the powers and duties of that officer. At all other times he may perform such duties as may be assigned him by the Grand Commandery or Grand Commander ; and he is required, either in person or by proxy, to attend all meetings of the Grand Encampment.

III.

Of the Grand Generalissimo and Grand Captain General.

The Grand Generalissimo and the Grand Captain General, in the absence of their superiors from any Conclave, shall severally take command, in the order of their rank ; and in the event of the death, removal from the State, or inability to serve, from any cause, of their superiors, shall in like manner succeed to and be charged with all the powers and duties of the Grand Commander. At all other times they shall perform such duties as may be assigned them by the Grand Commandery or Grand Commander ; and they are required, either in person or by proxy, to attend all meetings of the Grand Encampment.

IV.

Of the Grand Treasurer.

The Grand Treasurer shall receive all moneys belonging to the Grand Commandery from the Grand Recorder, and shall pay the same out under such regulations as by it may be provided. He shall keep a just record thereof in proper books, and at each Annual Conclave shall present a detailed account of his receipts and disbursements, together with vouchers for the last, and a full statement of the existing condition of the finances. He shall execute and file with the Grand Recorder, within fifteen days after his installation, a bond, in such terms, in such penal sum, and with such sureties as shall be approved by the Grand Commander, conditioned that he will faithfully discharge the duties of his office.

V.

Of the Grand Recorder.

The Grand Recorder shall keep an accurate record of all the transactions of the Grand Commandery which should be written. He shall collect the revenue and pay it over to the Grand Treasurer. He shall present a detailed report of his receipts, and of all business appertaining to his office, at each Annual Conclave. He shall, as soon as practicable, after each Annual Conclave, transmit copies of the transactions thereat to the Grand Master of the Order, the Grand Recorder of the Grand Encampment, the Grand Recorders of the several Grand Commanderies under the jurisdiction of that Body, and the Recorders of the several Commanderies within this jurisdiction. He shall keep the seal of the Grand Commandery, and shall affix it, with his attestation, to all instruments emanating from that Body, and to all dispensations issued by the Grand Commander. He shall conduct the correspondence of the Grand Commandery, and shall present, at each Annual Conclave, a summary of such proceedings of other Grand Commanderies as may have come into his possession. He shall transmit quarterly to each subordinate Commandery a list of all rejections, suspensions, expulsions, or restorations by the various Commanderies of the jurisdiction which shall have been received by him. He shall report, at each Annual Conclave, all unfinished business, and shall perform such other duties as may be assigned him by the Grand Commandery or Grand Commander. He shall receive such compensation for his services as the Grand Commandery may direct ; and shall execute and file with the Grand Treasurer, within fifteen days after his installation, a bond, in such terms, in such penal sum, and with such sureties as shall be approved by the Grand Commander, conditioned that he will faithfully discharge the duties of his office.

VI.

Of the other Grand Officers.

The duties of the remaining Grand Officers shall be such as traditionally appertain to their respective stations, and shall correspond, as nearly as may be, to those of the officers of similar rank in the Grand Encampment. In case all the four principal Grand Officers shall be absent from any Conclave, the Past Grand Officers of like rank shall, in the order of their rank and seniority, be empowered to take command.

CHAPTER III.

RELATIVE TO SUBORDINATE COMMANDERIES.

I.

Upon the petition of nine or more Knights Templar in good standing, the Grand Commandery, or the Grand Commander, may issue a Letter of Dispensation, authorizing them to form and open a Commandery of Knights Templar, to confer the Orders, and to receive members by affiliation. But no such dispensation shall issue unless the petition be accompanied by a recommendation from the Commandery nearest the location of the proposed new one, which shall certify to the good standing of each of the petitioners, to the proper qualifications of the officers whom they have nominated, and that a suitable place of assembling has been provided. Such dispensation shall terminate on the first day of the month in which the next succeeding Annual Conclave shall be holden, and then shall be returned to the Grand Recorder, together with the book of records, by-laws, and returns to that date, when, if the transactions of the new Commandery shall appear satisfactory to the Grand Commandery, it may, upon petition therefor, receive a charter.

II.
Of whom Composed.

A Commandery consists of a Commander, (whose address is *Eminent*), a Generalissimo, a Captain General, a Prelate, a Senior Warden, a Junior Warden, a Treasurer, a Recorder, a Standard Bearer, a Sword Bearer, a Warder, a Captain of the Guards, (the Sentinel), three Guards, and as many members as may be found convenient for work or discipline.

III.
Of Assemblies.

Each Commandery should hold a stated Assembly at least once in each month, for the transaction of its regular business ; but no action upon petitions for the orders or for affiliation shall be had until the expiration of at least four weeks after their reception. Special meetings may be ordered by the Commander, at his discretion, but no business shall be done thereat other than that specified in the order. A failure to assemble for six successive months shall be deemed sufficient cause for the arrest or revocation of its charter.

IV.
Of Elections.

The officers of each Commandery (except the Standard Bearer, the Sword Bearer, the Warder, the Sentinel, and the Guards, who shall be appointed by the Commander), shall be chosen by ballot at the first stated Assembly in the month of December in each year, and shall be installed before or at the next stated Assembly. A majority of all the votes cast shall be necessary for a choice.

V.
Of Voting.

All questions in a Commandery shall be determined by a majority of votes. Each member present shall be entitled to one vote, and when the votes are equally divided (except in elections), the Commander shall, in addition, have the casting vote.

VI.
Of Qualifications for the Orders.

No Commandery shall confer an Order of Knighthood upon any one who is not a regular Royal Arch Mason, according to the requirements of the General Grand Chapter of the United States of America, nor unless he shall have produced evidence of his good standing at the time of application ; and no application for the orders shall be received by any Commandery from one who, within six months next preceding, shall have been rejected by any Commandery (unless by dispensation from the Grand Commander), nor unless the applicant shall have resided one year next preceding in this State, and three months next preceding within its jurisdiction, except by permission of the Commandery nearest his place of residence.

VII.

Of Fees and Dues.

No Commandery shall confer the several Orders of Knighthood for a less fee than sixty dollars, and no application therefor shall be received unless accompanied by such fee. The dues of the members of each Commandery shall be such as may be provided in its by-laws, and the non-payment of such dues for a period of six months, unless good reason therefor be shown, shall be punished by suspension.

VIII.

Of the Commander.

Each Commander has it in special charge to see that the By-Laws of his Commandery, the Statutes and Orders of the Grand Commandery, and the Constitution and Regulations of the Grand Encampment are duly observed by the Knights under his command ; that accurate records are kept, and just accounts and proper reports rendered by his officers, and that regular returns are annually made to the Grand Commandery at the time prescribed therefor, with prompt payment of the annual dues. From his decision there shall be no appeal to the Commandery, but any five members thereof may complain of his decisions or conduct, to the Grand Commandery or Grand Commander. It shall be his duty, either in person or by proxy, to attend all Conclaves of the Grand Commandery.

IX.

Of the Generalissimo and Captain General.

The Generalissimo and Captain General shall perform the duties severally assigned them by the traditional usages of the Order ; and, in the absence of the Commander, shall, in the order of their rank, succeed to and be charged with all his powers and duties. It shall be the duty of both, either in person, or by proxy, to attend all Conclaves of the Grand Commandery. In the absence of all the three principal officers, the Past Commanders, in the order of their seniority, may take command.

X.

Of the Treasurer and Recorder.

The Treasurer shall receive from the Recorder, and safely keep, all moneys belonging to the Commandery ; and shall pay the same out under such regulations, and account therefor at such times and in such manner, as by it may be prescribed. The Recorder shall keep an accurate record of all the transactions of the Commandery, which should be written, including a list of the officers, members, and visitors present at each Assembly; shall collect the revenue and pay it over to the Treasurer ; shall keep correct accounts of the dues of members ; shall prepare and transmit the annual returns to the Grand Recorder ; shall keep the seal of the Commandery, and affix it to all documents emanating therefrom ; and shall perform such other duties as may be required of him by the Commandery or Commander.

XI.

Of Returns.

The Returns of each Commandery shall be made up to the first day of February in each year, in such form as shall be prescribed by the Grand Commandery ; and shall immediately be forwarded to the Grand Recorder with the dues as hereinbefore provided.

CHAPTER IV.

MISCELLANEOUS.

I.

Of Trials and Appeals.

The mode of proceeding in all trials shall, as nearly as may be, be that which is now or may be hereafter prescribed in the Regulations of the Grand Lodge of Free and Accepted Masons of this State ; and appeals from the results of such trials may, in like manner as is directed by the Grand Lodge, be made to and adjudicated by the Grand Commandery.

II.

Of Penalties.

Censure, suspension, or expulsion may be inflicted by any Commandery upon any Knight within its jurisdiction, for unknightly conduct, or for violation of, or disobedience to any of the By-Laws, Statutes, Orders, Regulations, or Constitutions of the Order. Information of a suspension or expulsion by any Commandery shall immediately be communicated by its Recorder to the Grand Recorder ; but no publication thereof shall be made except by the Grand Commandery. Suspension may be removed by the Commandery which imposed it, but an expelled Knight can only be restored by the Grand Commandery.

III.

Of Vows of Office.

All Officers of the Grand Commandery and of its subordinates, before entering upon the duties of their respective stations, shall take a solemn vow that they will maintain and support the Constitution and Regulations of the Grand Encampment of Knights Templar of the United States of America, and the Statutes and Orders of the Grand Commandery of the State of California.

IV.

Of Amendments.

The Statutes may be altered or amended at any Annual Conclave by the votes of two-thirds of the members present.

GENERAL REGULATIONS

OF THE

GRAND COMMANDERY OF CALIFORNIA.

1. That the Grand Recorder be instructed to procure the portrait of each retiring Grand Commander, and have it placed with those heretofore ordered by the Grand Commandery. [October, 1867.]

2. That the officers of the Grand Commandery of California be required to present themselves for duty at any of its sessions, equipped in the uniform prescribed by the Grand Encampment of the United States. [April, 1874.]

3. That the *members* of the Grand Commandery of the State of California be required to appear at its Annual Conclave, clothed in the uniform of the Order as worn by their respective Commanderies. [April, 1875.]

4. That each Commander of a subordinate Commandery of this State be required to open and close his Commandery in accordance with the drill and lecture this day adopted. [April, 1878.]

5. That the several subordinate Commanderies of this jurisdiction be requested to assemble in their respective Asylums on Good Friday, Easter, and Ascension day of each year, and proceed in a body from thence to some place of public worship, for Divine service; and in case no place of public worship can be had, then such service shall be held in the Asylum of their said Commanderies. [April, 1879 and 1883.]

6. That in order to be in good standing as a Knight Templar, it is necessary to be in good standing as a Master Mason, as such standing is defined by the laws of the Grand Lodge of this State. [April, 1880.]

7. That all Red Cross Knights, before they shall receive the Order of the Temple, shall be subjected to an examination in open Commandery, or before a special committee of three Sir Knights, and be declared or reported proficient in the manual of the sword, facings, marching, and the cuts, signs, grip, and words of the illustrious Order of Red Cross Knights. [April, 1880.]

8. That the Recorders of subordinate Commanderies be required to add to the Annual Reports made to the Grand Commandery, the number of regulation uniforms belonging to their respective Commanderies, and to the individual members thereof. [April, 1881.]

9. That applications for a waiver of jurisdiction over candidates for the orders of Knighthood shall be read in open Commandery at least four weeks previous to a vote being had thereon ; and such waiver shall only be granted on the unanimous vote of the Sir Knights present who are members of the Commandery to which the application is made. [April, 1882.]

10. That it shall be deemed unknightly conduct in any Sir Knight who shall importune or solicit any companion to apply for the orders of Knighthood, or for admission, to any Commandery. [April, 1882.]

11. That dispensations to enable a Commandery to re-ballot for a candidate, and to shorten the time for taking such ballot upon the application of a companion, be issued by the Grand Recorder, upon the order of the $R.\therefore E.\therefore$ Grand Commander, and under the seal of the Grand Commandery, and that a fee of five dollars be paid therefor to the Grand Recorder. [April, 1884.]

That applications for leave to contribute shall in every case be sent to the Society of which such contributor is a member, and the Committee, at least fourteen days before a vote being had thereon, shall send notice that at least one-fourth ... the approbation of the Committee present whose members of the Society by which the application is made. [April 1882.]

That it shall be lawful for any Society to exercise all the rights ... than pecuniary to enable any person to apply for the grant of relief ... money given where necessary accordingly. [April 1882.]

... the same to the said Committee in ... that ... shall thereupon ... expression amended by original regulation, and the rules of the ... and determined, and make the said rules ... for temporary and that ... that the contributor shall be able to ... and thereon. [April 1882.]

INDEX.

H

I

J

M